THE

~~RUDGE PARK~~

the inbetweeners

~~COMPREHENSIVE~~

YEARBOOK

Published by Century 2011

2 4 6 8 10 9 7 5 3 1

First published in Great Britain in 2011 by Century
Random House, 20 Vauxhall Bridge Road,
London SW1V 2SA

www.randomhouse.co.uk

Addresses for companies within The Random House Group Limited can be found at: www.randomhouse.co.uk

The Random House Group Limited Reg. No. 954009

A CIP catalogue record for this book is available from the British Library

ISBN 9781846059278

Printed and bound in China

Design by Tony Lyons and Kate Stretton for Estuary English – www.estuaryenglish.co.uk.
Illustrations by Will Mower

Pictures supplied by Getty Images, iStockphoto, Shutterstock.
Every reasonable effort has been made to contact the copyright holders, but if there are any errors or omissions, Century will be pleased to insert the appropriate acknowledgment in any subsequent printing.

THE

RUDGE PARK

the inbetweeners

COMPREHENSIVE

YEARBOOK

Edited by William McKenzie

CENTURY

Rudge Park yearbook

EDITOR'S NOTE

Welcome pupils from Rudge Park Upper Sixth Form, welcome parents, welcome, of course, our esteemed teachers, and welcome to the scores of casual readers who may have a connection with the school, or are just fans of good journalism and may have picked up this book. You are very welcome.

Welcome all.

So, as I say, welcome to the first ever Rudge Park yearbook. When I started at the school I knew I'd be bringing some new ideas, shaking a few things up a bit, changing stuff for the better, and I hope you agree that this yearbook is one of those things.

A few bits of housekeeping before we start. Not apologies – housekeeping. The first thing to note is that due to a print deadline that I can, with no hyperbole, only describe as fascistic, you may find that some of the book doesn't flow as well as it should. This, as I say, is simply due to the "people" at the printers saying that because of the deal they gave us (although it didn't seem much of a deal) we had to have the book ready to print on the exact date we had given them. Admittedly, they did give us a two-week extension to that deadline, but sometimes when you are dealing with art, as I tried to tell them, deadlines are unhelpful. Anyway as I say, housekeeping and not an apology, but it does mean that the flow may not be exactly what I was looking for and, possibly more crucially, some articles, items, adverts or some pieces of random paper may have unintentionally been included. Some, not a lot. Some. It does not spoil the book, no matter what my mother says.

Good. Well, welcome (have I said welcome yet? If not, "welcome") dear reader and whilst it may not be Orwell, I humbly hope you enjoy my first foray into the written word. And also enjoy the contributions of some others. But if it does sound a bit like Orwell that bit will probably have been me because I've been reading a lot of Orwell recently.

So, welcome, and enjoy.

William McKenzie

Editor

Rudge Park yearbook

INTRODUCTION

Hello, and welcome to the first ever – and I presume last ever – Rudge Park leavers "yearbook". Personally I think we absorb enough pointless transatlantic marketing ideas without having to go looking for another, but here we are.

This is where I find myself in my fortieth year, writing the introduction to something no one has ever cared about before, or missed, and arguably in the age of facebooks and Twitters has less point and relevance than ever. I find myself asking, what is it about US culture that's so pervasive, so "cool", that the pupils not just under my charge, but under all the put-upon, overworked and underpaid sixth form heads throughout the country, feel the need to ape it. The "prom"? The "prom"? We already had "sixth form dances" (or "balls" if you went to that sort of school); there was no need for the Yankee rebrand other than to make it seem more glamorous. Well, I've travelled to Detroit for a family wedding, and let me tell you there is nothing glamorous about it at all, unless I was tricked and Jimmy Choo have started making new "plastic bag" shoes and Armani do a range of thick, piss-smelling coats to be worn under even larger, even more malodorous woollen jumpers.

But I digress. This "yearbook" (for God's sake) has been put together by the students. And when I say the students I mean one in particular, whose idea the whole enterprise was. Will Mckenzie has worked hard, I presume, to get contributions from all his fellow leavers this year, but even a cursory glance through the fetid pages of this "book" will show you that he obviously didn't work hard enough. I've not read it at all, nor do I intend to, but from what I've seen whilst it was passed under my eyes the whole thing is a mess, a hotch potch formed in desperation I suspect the night before it was due at the printers. This was the night I found Mckenzie in the common room, at midnight (what I was doing there doesn't matter) slumped over various random sheets of paper, pictures and forms, weeping. Yes, weeping, like a panicking little baby, because he couldn't make sense of the book and all the submissions he'd been given.

Did I abandon him? No, I did not.

After I'd stopped laughing, I scooped up all the papers spread out on the desk, put them in a pile and just took them to the printers as they were.

What was in there? I don't know.

What order are they in? I don't care.

But what I do know is that if this were a paid enterprise I'd deserve the lion's share. Without my timely intervention, this thing I don't care about would never have happened.

And that's just one example of how I put myself out for the pupils of Rudge Park this year. And what thanks do I get in return? I get called into the head's office and told "please look after the 'yearbook', it seems a great idea".

I doubt anyone is still reading this but if you are, see this book for what it is - a cry for help from a lonely young man.

All the best, toodle pip,

P. Gilbert

Mr Phillip Gilbert, BA HONS
Head of Sixth Form

Simon Cooper

Yearbook profile

I just asked Will what he wrote for his yearbook page to get an idea of what stuff we should be writing here and he said he talked about what he'd learnt at Rudge Park. So I might as well do the same. In my 7 years here, I've learnt lots of things about English, Maths, Biology, German, Chemistry, Geography, P.E., Physics, Sociology and General Studies. But then I suppose that's the same as everyone really, because that's what school's for, isn't it?

Will also said I could use this as an opportunity to thank my friends who've supported me during my time at Rudge Park. But I'm not sure I've got any friends who have supported me, really. I've got friends, obviously, like Jay, Neil and Will. So thanks to them for being friends, but that's all.

I suppose one person who has supported me at school, because we've known each other since we were 8 and she's been there for me even before my very first day here, is probably Carli D'Amato. In a way, because we've known each other for so long, I probably know her better than anyone ever will, and she knows me better than anyone ever will too. So thanks Carli! Who knows, we might even end up at the same uni together by some weird coincidence! (Wouldn't that be totally strange and unplanned by either of us if that actually happened? It'd be mental! But brilliant. Brilliantly mental.)

I suppose people probably thank their parents in these kinds of articles too, but that's not really appropriate in my case. If anything, they've held me back quite a bit and distracted me from stuff with the ridiculous family catastrophes they've caused, and their stupid rules about speed limits and what time people can stay out till and internet access – I was only looking for new underwear.

I'll leave with certain memories of this place. And I'm sure everyone will leave with certain memories of me too. Just so no one goes away with false memories though, I would like to get it on record that the incident I had at the Fashion Show was absolutely not my fault. I was rushed onto the catwalk, and the costume was quite small, and Neil Sutherland was supposed to be checking for wardrobe malfunctions. Probably best to draw a line under it all now as we're moving on and can leave this kind of baggage behind.

So that's it basically. Cheers.

Best moment: My exam revision sessions. Sounds weird, I know, but I had a really good revision partner who actually made revising fun, even in subjects I wasn't doing.

Most likely to: Don't know really. I'll just see how things go, I suppose.

Nickname: Si (just a shortening of my name, really). *STATUE OF LIBERTY (his hair)*

Awards: I'm quite good at golf, nearly good enough to win an award until my friends bullied me into giving up..

"most likely to use up the world's supply of hair gel!"

↓

"Owner of the world's shittest car"

↓

"Swanage's best naked sailor"

fit → not as good as Simon!

Walking round with my bollock out at the Fashion Show

WILLS MUM LOOKS FIT IN A THONG

Carli D'Amato

Yearbook profile

Writing this is so weird, because I can't believe my time at Rudge Park is nearly over! It only seems like yesterday since my first day here. Back then I only knew two people (Rachel and Simon C) but it wasn't long before everyone in the year wanted to be friends and I didn't need to cling to my primary school friends anymore (though obviously Rachel remained my bezzie mate all the way through – love ya Rach!).

While there have been many magical school moments which will stay with me forever, there is one event which stands out from the rest. The Charity Fashion Show. It began as a tiny acorn of an idea in my mind. Having heard of Alistair Scott's terrible illness, I thought to myself "What can I / we all do to help those less fortunate than myself / ourselves?" Initially, I considered lots of potential fundraising methods: sponsored walks, marathon running, parachute jumping. But all of them seemed rather inefficient ways of raising money (as well as being uninteresting to organise, a bit clichéd, and uninteresting to young people). So I thought about what skills I could use to raise funds, and it hit me: fashion!

And that's how the Charity Fashion Show was born. What followed was simply overwhelming. From my tiny idea, a huge school-wide event flourished. On that night, some original and glamorous clothing changed the world for the better. Just a little bit. And that's a bit like what I learnt at this school. With good ideas and hard work, I know we can all become wonderful and make the world better, whilst wearing really cool clothes.

This school has given me so much to me, and this yearbook seems the best place to share with everyone exactly how it has shaped who I am today. So finally, to summarise my life at the school, this is what Rudge Park means to me:

Really good friends who will stay in my life forever.

Unbelievable feeling after helping those less fortunate than me at the Charity Fashion show.

Dialysis machine – what the money we raised very nearly paid for.

Glamorous Nights fashion collection. My exquisite designs made real.

Excellent teachers helping out that the charity show – thanks Mr Kennedy!

Partying with everyone who's anyone in Donovan's room in Swanage.

A-Level revision with my friend, Simon C. Friends forever.

Rach! Best friends forever. Our nights out at the Astoria – legendary!

Krazy nights out that helped me meet my man Tom. Love ya babe!

Best moment: When I found out how much the Charity Fashion Show had raised to help buy a dialysis machine for St. Margaret's hospital. We made £523! After expenses, that meant there was £76 leftover for St. Margaret's. I can't imagine how many dialysis machies they got for that. So amazing and humbling.

Most likely to: Become a fashion designer and / or write for *Heat* Magazine! Or just work for a really worthwhile charity.

Nickname: The boys used to call me Carli Tomato (cos of D'Amato...) but that ended about the same time I stopped wearing braces and started wearing make-up.

Awards: Feels a bit showy-offy to put anything here. Some people have made suggestions – like Alistair Scott said I could put Most Selfless Babe here. Hilarious!

Told you, you've got no chance

Neil Sutherland

Yearbook profile

So Will says we've all got a page to do whatever we want with in this yearbook which is amazing because I don't think I've ever had a page to do whatever I want with before. As soon as he said it I had had a load of amazing ideas about what to do with it, but now I'm actually doing it I've totally forgotten what they all were. That can happen sometimes when you've got loads of stuff in your head like me. Forgetting stuff actually happens to me quite a lot.

What else? My name's Neil. I like drawing and Jay says I'm pretty good at it, not as good as him but I might be good enough to draw a comic or a Pixar film or something. I'll do a drawing now. Wait there:

I nearly never came back for extra school cos I had a job lined up – going into business with Jay. He was setting up a detective agency that only did work for massive Hollywood stars. I was gonna be the muscle but he said there was a problem with our green cards and we couldn't go to America. So we decided to do more school. Dunno why really cos I forgot how boring it was. Even Additional PE was rubbish. I know, who'd have thought that? There was only two of us in the class, me and Big John. If you think he stinks just sitting in the common room you should get a whiff of his rank BO after an hour of running about. He doesn't even like PE, he said he only did it to try and make his dad happy. He could've just bought some Lynx instead of spending two years getting hammered by me at table tennis.

Best moment: The bit in *Fast and Furious 3: Tokyo Drift* when he pulls a skid up that car park ramp. It's amazing, I've watched it like a thousand times.

Weirdest bit was having to sit on Mr Kennedy's lap during detention because he said all the school's chairs had been sent off to get fixed. I still wonder how all the chairs other than his managed to be broken on the same day. Like I said, weird.

William Mackenzie

Yearbook profile

If I've learnt only one thing from my time at Rudge Park (and it is possible that I've genuinely only learnt ONE THING, even after being subjected to what they call lessons for the past two years), it's that however retro and "old-school" it may seem, a wedgie still hurts.

You'd assume that it would be the arse crack that would bear the brunt, but funnily enough (or rather, seriously enough, in my case), it's actually the squashing of the gonads at the front of the pants are pulled back and under that really causes the sharp pain.

But, I suppose, I have taken in (I'm sorry, I know this is meant to be a valedictory page, but it's late and "learnt" really is too strong a word) a couple of other life lessons. As I may have mentioned (it is late, isn't is?) these are not of the academic variety.

The first is that reinvention is possibly harder than invention. That might sound wrong, but I'd suggest that unless you've tried it, you won't understand. Which leads me on to the second thing I've possibly come to realise (I simply refuse to say "learn" about anything that in any way relates to this place. The school Rudge Park. I'm so tired, what time IS IT?):

The second is that if you don't try, you don't get anything. I tried to raise our status in the school and, yes, I suppose, especially in the eyes of the female contingent – and I think from my perspective (admittedly a late night, blurry-eyed one) – I think I succeeded. Broadly. Look, okay, maybe girls aren't crazy about people who are ill through no fault of their own in exams, or who unwittingly insult recently bereaved medicated giants, but how's this for a roll of honour:

Prom Organizer

Duke of Edinburgh Award organizer

And that's just the start. Or is it the end? Either way I really need to go to bed, but first I'll just try to get together this book. Right, page one. I don't need to write down what I'm thinking, do i? No. Great. Hmm, still doing it. Oh shit, haven't finished this yet, and look at the other sections. Right, do that first, then cross out that profanity above, then finish collating and editing the whole yearbook before 7am tomorrow.

Best moment: I think, looking back on it (obviously, it's not happening as I type. No, not by a long chalk. What does that mean? I am so tired) the best moment was either the whole experience and what I learnt about myself, friendship and others or when Charlotte Hinchcliffe tongued me.

Worst moment: Well, I mean it's obvious. Or is it? Yes, no, it is. I was ill. ILL. In an exam. If I'd had cancer in that exam or my leg had blown off, they wouldn't call me CheMo Mowlam or Heather McCartney would they? And it's exactly the same thing.

Most likely to: If we're talking about me, then "succeed". And that's not bragging, that's just true. Out of this sixth form I am the most likely to succeed because the competition is so low. The most likely thing to happen to this page, though, is that someone will draw a cock on my photo. I'd say pretty much guaranteed, not "likely".

Awards: What does that mean? I created this form, why have I put this on here? I KNOW nobody has any awards. What was I expecting: "Oh yeah, I've got five Oscars, a Grammy and an Olympic silver in boxing?" No, no awards. Obviously. That cannot be the right time. WHY ARE THERE NO WORKING CLOCKS?????

John Webster

Yearbook profile

Firstly, thank you to my good friend and starting buddy Will McKenzie for asking me to write on this page. Also apologies to Will McKenzie for the bits of McFlurry that have ended up on the page. (It's the Lion Bar McFlurry – I hope that in the future, I'll remember which month I wrote this. Next month it's Cornetto flavour.)

When I joined the school I didn't feel like I really fitted in. But over the last few terms I feel like I have really bonded with one person in particular – my counsellor. He gets me. As for the students, while I have offered olive branches to several of them, I have so far had few takers. As a result, I prefer to spend time on my own, without all that social pressure. I don't need to fit in either; I'm much happier with a paint brush in my hand. Or a cheesestring. If any of my peers are bothering to read this I would like to point out that they are only rude to me because they are frustrated with themselves. And frustration often comes from wanting to be noticed. My counsellor's wise words, not mine.

When I leave I don't think I will keep in contact with anyone here (apart from, perhaps, Jay Cartwright. Jay, I'm still waiting for you to accept me on Facebook. I know it's probably because you haven't logged in for a while, so maybe you should log in now?).

I am very much looking forward to going to university. I see it as a new beginning. A chance to meet some proper friends. Some people like me. When I get there, I'm going to float the nickname "Awesome John". It never caught on here, sadly. "Awesome John" will be a party animal with a washboard stomach. I am going to go swimming over the holidays to achieve this. Also, my cousin has promised to teach me how to play "Run" by Snow Patrol on the guitar, so that will surely help to make me more popular in a uni environment. I am also going to start wearing jeans with chains on and a neck scarf.

I did have some good times at Rudge Park. Like, I enjoyed being put in charge of the food at the school Christmas prom. We had burgers. Although I did briefly wonder about having lasagne. But lasagne can fall off the plate. So I went with burgers.

As well as the prom I also enjoyed my fair share of house parties (I consider two to be my "fair share"). Louise's was best because a girl spoke to me and things got a bit fruity. Still haven't heard from her. But she's probably just not read any of my emails, texts, tweets, Facebook messages or Bebo requests. Perhaps she uses MySpace instead of all those things. I'll try her on that.

In conclusion? Well, Rudge Park has been a microcosm of my life. I arrived on my own and I'm going to leave on my own. But I do think I've grown at Rudge Park. I think I am a stronger person than when I started. I am worried about moving on. I'm going to miss school dinners and I worry about university dinner. Will they be any better? Or worse? Who knows? But it's something I look forward to finding out.

John.

Best moment: Getting fruity with a girl at Louise's party and bonding with Jay at the Christmas Prom.

Most likely to: Everyone says I'm the student most likely to go postal. But I don't want to be a postman.

Nickname: "Big John" and "Awesome John" (only I use the latter). Although my counsellor says nicknames are negative reinforcements and I shouldn't listen to them.

Awards: I asked Jay what award I should win. He said if I went on a diet I could be "The Biggest Loser". He then said I could be called that even if I didn't go on a diet. I love his "banter".

Jay Cartwright

Yearbook profile

Will I miss Rudge Park? Stupid question really. Course I won't. It's a bit like asking Wayne Rooney if he'd rather be being sat in a classroom trying to make maths work in his stupid fat head, or be drinking Cristal from his Golden Boot while having a massive orgy with seventeen unbelievable fitties that all have to call him Sir Wayne. Because that is what successful people (me in the future) do. So no, I won't bloody miss this place. I will miss Neil though.

Best time? Definitely the Xmas ball organised by myself and a little bit by Will. It was great for two reasons. One, I DJd so the roof was on fire. Two, I got a blowie behind the decks by a girl who looked like a much fitter, less pikier version of Tulisa from N-Dubz. Class.

If I had to pass on one piece of advice to the new sixth formers it would be this – try not to pork all the vadge by the first half term break. It's a long two years so you need to pace yourself. Believe me. Once you've had all of the available school clunge then you have to move onto porn stars, models and TV presenters. While this sounds amazing, which it absolutely is, it does require a lot of time and effort and ultimately your A-levels will suffer. But who gives a fuck? When will I ever use A-levels in the future. But I also had a threesome with Fearne Cotton and Kate Moss so it's swings and roundabouts really.

One day in the future when I'm a head of my multi-billion business empire built on my DJing and football activities I will come back and do a talk about how awesome it is to be born for greatness. So see you losers next year then!

THE J-CART ENTERTAINMENT CORPORATION PRESENTS

STRUM

D-JAY CARTWRIGHT

DAVID GUETTA DAFT PUNK
BASSHUNTER
MARK RONSON FATBOY SLIM
JUDGE JULES GROOVERIDER
ARMAND VAN HELDEN ERIC MORILLO

LIVE P.A. FROM LUCY PINDER
INDIE ROOM - DJ SETS FROM LIAM GALLAGHER,
ZANE LOWE AND KURT COBAIN

EARLY BIRD TICKETS: £50
buy directly from Jay Cartwright or Neil Sutherland, cash only.
TICKETS ON THE DOOR: £100 (before 11pm), £250 (once D-Jay
Cartwright's set has begun)
FITTIE PRICE: £5 for all fitties, as judged by Jay Cartwright (not
Neil Sutherland).

31ST DECEMBER 2010
4.00PM TO 3.00AM
THE O2 ARENA, LONDON

Neil, I've done the flyer on my computer, so now I need you to call up all the people listed on it to check they're available. While you're at it, you might as well call the O2 and find out how much room hire is and if you need a deposit or extension leads or anything. I would do the phoning, but I ran out of credit. Nice one! STRUM is going to be huge!!.

Jay

HELLO! I'M WILL

AND I'M DOING A SHIT.

Mark Donovan
Yearbook profile

Briefcase has told me I can write whatever I want in my yearbook piece, so F██k. B██ks. Moth██ker. W██kers. Let's see how much of that makes the final edition. And he's said I can have any picture I want on my page too. Well I'm going for the one of Briefcase on the bog. And if he doesn't print it, then he'll be an enemy against freedom of speech.

Now I just want to wrap this up with a few quick shout outs. Thanks to the posse: Big Moe C, Booley Booley, the Wildman and Egg. Respect to my boyz. Big love to all the Rudge Park ladies who I've been with; and you're welcome. Shout out to Briefcase's mum Polly (you'll probably read this cos you're that kind of mum) and I just want to say keep in touch cos now I'm leaving school, the game has totally changed. Finally, to that manky-haired French exchange kid who stayed at Cooper's house – if you ever come to the UK, or if you even set foot on a P&O ferry again, I guarantee that I will kill you.

Peace out.

Best moment: Making Briefcase wear a bin on his head.

Nickname: "Donovan". That's the only option. Though if anyone's got any clever ideas for other nicknames they want to call me, then feel free to come and suggest them to me face-to-face and I promise to give them an honest and instant reaction.

Awards: The F██ing best!

THE RUDGE PARK YEAR IN PHOTOGRAPHS

By WILLIAM MCKENZIE

Yearbook Editor

As a wise man once said – *"a picture paints a thousand words"*

So with that in mind, what better way to chronicle life in Rudge Park over the last two years than by a collection of stirring and memorable photographs? Following my open invitation to the upper sixth to send in their favourite snaps (later widened to the lower sixth as well due to the disappointing response, and then subsequently the whole school, including staff and people who lived nearby and with the deadline extended on six occasions), the images below represent the widest possible selection of contributions received. So thank you to everyone who submitted a photo. Except for Jay Cartwright – I'm not printing any of those. Unfortunately, due to other time pressures with regard to the yearbook I was unable to complete this section and so handed over editorial duties to Mr. Kennedy.

"Thanks Will, I was delighted to be able to use this opportunity to showcase my own love of photography, especially long lens shots." – Mr. Kennedy.

YUM! That's pudding. Submitted by: Big John

CHRISTMAS PROM A student loses his inhibitions in front of onlooking teaching staff.
Submitted by: Mr. Kennedy

INSIGNIFICANCE The Eta Carina Nebula reminds us that Earth is merely a drop in the cosmic ocean.
Taken with my Orion 420 Telescope Camera. Submitted by: Susie McGivern

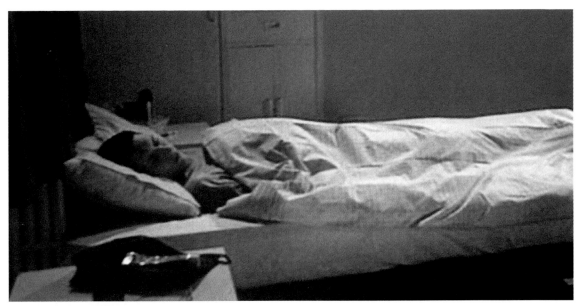

THE SWANAGE FIELD TRIP A student relaxes after a busy day, utterly vulnerable.
Submitted by: Mr. Kennedy

GEOLOGICAL FEATURE A classic chalk headland showing softer primarily Wealdon clay striations
and evidence of quarrying. Submitted by: Mr. Kennedy

Left:
REFURBISHED SPORTS
HALL CHANGING ROOMS
These are much more
aesthetically pleasing than
the older ones.
Submitted by: Mr. Kennedy

Below:
LATE NIGHT HOMEWORK
A student studies at home
into the early hours.
Submitted by: Mr. Kennedy

JUSTIN BIEBER A musical artist who achieved notable success during this academic year.
Submitted by: Mr. Kennedy

CHARITY FASHION SHOW A genuinely rousing occasion which turned me on to fashion.
Submitted by: Mr. Kennedy

ROLLERCOASTER!

Ttravel correspondent WILLIAM MCKENZIE

Dear fellow Rudge Park pupils,

It's a sad fact that only 2% of UK adults have ridden a roller coaster. Now I, for one, am doing my bit to bump up these statistics – although admittedly I am not, legally speaking, an adult quite yet (but I am very mature for my age and would probably count as an adult in most sorts of survey). But my point is, roller coasters are great fun and there are theme parks all over the UK with some truly world-class thrill rides. It might be that you've only visited the obvious ones: Thorpe Park, Chessington World of Adventures and the motherland, Alton Towers. If indeed this is the case, then you are what the Roller Coaster Enthusiasts of Great Britain Society would term a "casual coaster". That is, you ride roller coasters merely two or three times a year.

As a formerly very active member of the R.C.E.O.G.B.S., I however have been on literally dozens of "coasters" (as they're known in the club) and before turning sixteen had already achieved the rank of Coaster Connoisseur. As such a seasoned thrill-seeker, it would be pretty unfair of me not to share with all of you my knowledge of the best coasters in the world. That way, should you ever get the chance to venture beyond the two or three mainstream theme parks that your unimaginative parents have taken you to, you can seize that opportunity, safe in the knowledge you've got some connoisseur-level guidance to help you maximise your personal thrill-seeking.

And so here, whittled down from the 45 coasters I have ridden (including children's rides, admittedly) are my top five in the world. They're in roughly chronological order because that's just the way I remember them. And boy, do they bring back some memories!

INDIANA JONES ET LE TEMPLE DU PÉRIL
DISNEYLAND PARIS, FRANCE

Construction: **Steel**
Length: **599.8m**
Type: **Sit-down (mining train themed)**
Ride date: **16th April 2005**

My first ever proper roller coaster experience – and
on a steel track too! Of course I've been on dozens
of more thrilling coasters since then, but the Indiana
Jones ride retains a special place in my heart. I still
remember the hot-breathed anticipation of queuing for
three hours to take my first ride. So you can tell this
was back in the dark days before Fast Track ticketing!
But I've always said you can't beat a good queue. Dad
wanted to come on with me but Mum was too scared
so he took her on "It's A Small World" instead, and
they laughed and really enjoyed it and the whole park.

BIZARRO, SIX FLAGS NEW ENGLAND, USA

Construction: **Steel**
Length: **1.6km**
Type: **Sit-down**
Ride date: **31st July 2006**

From the breath-taking views of the Connecticut River to the classic Headchopper tunnel and exhilarating flame effects, the Bizarro is truly a feat of roller-coasting genius. And I'm not one of these people who just bandies the word "genius" about willy-nilly, trust me. Albert Einstein was a genius; Puff Daddy is not. But back to the coaster and it's no wonder that Bizarro has won the Golden Ticket Award (the coaster equivalent of the Riba Stirling award) for Best Steel Roller Coaster on no fewer than five occasions. I was fortunate enough to ride this coaster on a family road trip across America in 2006 – just me, Mum and Dad and the great open road! Although, looking back, it was more often than not just me and Mum and a motel room film because Dad spent quite a lot of time getting drunk in the motel bars. But Mum put a brave face on whatever issues they might have been having. But mostly I remember Bizarro; that roller coaster provided me with the single greatest thrill I have experienced to date. Sometimes, I doubt whether that high will ever be matched. But that's just an occupational hazard of riding coasters.

EXPEDITION GEFORCE, HOLIDAY PARK, GERMANY

Construction: **Steel**
Length: **1.22km**
Type: **Sit-down**
Ride date: **22nd October 2007**

I'd imagine you've never even heard of Haßloch, let alone the municipality's incredible amusement park, Holiday Park (ignore the terrible name). I'll admit, I was completely unaware of it too until I read of its Expedition GeForce roller coaster in the Summer '07 edition of the R.C.E.O.G.B.S.N.E.W.S. (the Roller Coaster Enthusiasts of Great Britain Society Newsletter). Shortly after, on a cultural holiday to Germany, I managed to persuade my parents to detour via Holiday Park. That wasn't easy. By then they were arguing pretty much constantly and they seemed to keep forgetting I was there. But I was OK with it. I just threatened to call ChildLine again and they soon went quiet. Anyway, with its initial 82° drop followed immediately by a 74° banking to the right and several big moments of air-time, you can certainly tell why they called it GeForce! While Dad didn't actually see me riding it, he did comment on how thrilling the ride looked from the bar next door. And after I told Mum about this Exocet missile of a coaster, I could tell she regretted staying in the car all day because of some texts she'd found on Dad's phone. But what a place. I think I'll always associate Germany with Holiday Park, Expedition GeForce, breaded meat products and shouting.

GOLIATH, WALIBI WORLD, NETHERLANDS

Construction: **Steel**
Length: **1.214km**
Type: **Sit-down**
Ride date: **25th October 2007**

On our drive back from the aforementioned trip to Germany (see Expedition GeForce overleaf), I was also able to convince Mum to stop off in the Dutch town of Biddinghuizen to further sate my thrill-seeking appetite on the Goliath at Walibi World. Dad wasn't travelling with us by this point. Because of some urgent work commitment, he'd caught a flight home and left us to make our own

way back. Which is how life was from then on really. Mum cried for two days, but that didn't stop her from taking my requested detour which was most definitely worth it. Not for nothing has this ride been described as "the fastest, highest and longest coaster in the Benelux" (I have tried to find a source to legitimise this quote, but unfortunately it remains unverified. I imagine the quote was originally in Dutch, French or Flemish, which has made it somewhat harder to pin down.) Highlights of the ride include an exhilarating 270° double helix AND a 380° upwards helix. I must confess to actually vomiting during this ride, but I put that entirely down to me losing my travel wristbands when Dad went berserk with the luggage at a Dutch service station, rather than the coaster itself inducing nausea. After all, us thrill-seekers have steel-lined stomachs by design! So next time you're in Biddinghuizen, do take in the Goliath. It was certainly more fun than witnessing my parents' marriage crumble into dust.

NEMESIS INFERNO, THORPE PARK, UNITED KINGDOM

Construction: **Steel**
Length: **750m**
Type: **Sit-down**
Ride date: **26th October 2008**

This one starts with the longest pre-lift section of any Bolliger-and-Mabillard-designed coaster in the world... and only gets better from there on in. It's got it all: an inverted track, a double loop, a zero-G rotation and even a double-interlocking corkscrew! For us professional thrill-seekers, that's a roller-coasting royal flush. Dad would probably have been proud but I don't really care what he thinks anymore because he left my mother and I to fend for ourselves and that's unforgivable. Fun fact: I've had the pleasure of riding Nemesis Inferno on the front row! Unfortunately I seem to have misplaced the photo of this particular experience. Such a shame.

So there you have it – my top five. Do "check them out" yourself, or why not come up with your own top five? I promise you won't be disappointed. Coast on!

Simon, are you sure you want to publish these under your name and using the real names?

My Poems

By Simon Cooper

I find poetry a great way to relax and express myself. Here are a few of my favourites, I hope you enjoy and are moved by them.

It's your fault

It's your fault, Mum and Dad, I didn't ask to be born
Everything you say makes me want to yawn
Other teenagers are allowed to drink beer and watch porn
Sometimes out of this family, I wish I could be torn.

Even though this is also my home
The thought-Nazi police won't leave me alone
Is it too much to ask to have a girl in my room
Without the door open, so she'll give me some poon?

So next time I stay out late at a club or somewhere
Or next time in front of your face I do swear
Or override the parental control software
Remember it's all your fault, and you're being well unfair.

I know of a prick

I know of a prick, his name is Tom
I can't fucking wait till he is gone
Off to university or a gap year instead
I genuinely don't mind if he soon gets dead.

I know of a prick, his name is Tom
Why did he have to turn up to the stupid prom?
I thought he had dumped her, I thought I was in
But now instead of mine, she's now touching his thing.

I know of a prick, his name is Tom
He thinks he's so cool, but he's a rugby mong
Underneath his car I'd like to stick a bomb
And when it blew him up I'd comfort Carli with my dong.

I know of a prick, his name is Tom
And I'm serious, it's not on
That he shags the girl I love with his stupid dick
In summary: Tom is a prick.

For Hannah

I will never forget you, dear Hannah
For the way you tugged at my love spanner
Even though it hurt quite a bit
When I was kicked in the penis by that little shit.

But I know that a kick to my erection
Was never really your intention
To make me come was all you planned
To make me come, all over your hand.

I wish you'd have finished me with your touch
Sadly my knob was hurting too much.
But I shall never forget your hand shuffling in my jeans
On that erotic night at the disco for under-eighteens.

Of Lauren

Lauren, we met
It wasn't a bet

We had a hug
And you must have felt the growth in my bug
By bug I mean my penis
You may also have felt its freeness
It really bounced around
When your cuddles I had found.

You had to move on because your dad's in the army
I just think that's bloody barmy
But that is the nature of war
Why must man hate man and fight?
And why must your Dad get moved to a different camp when I was going
to get to kiss you? Hugs are nice, but kisses are better
And like I'm sure you know kisses lead to more
Though I'm not saying you're a whore.*

---

* Maybe leave off whore line - what do you think Will?

Carli's poem

I've known a girl for a very long time
I am determined to make her mine
This girl's name is called Carli
And I've been chasing her near and far-li.

Over her little brother I did once up-chuck
Oh dear God I really want her to fuck.

When I was young I yearned for a filly
She made me feel all warm and silly
I dreamt of her when nights were chilly
Which made me get a lovely stiffy.

Ode to Tara

There once was a girl called Tara

Who I first kissed in a bar-a

I liked her look

And the taste of her puke

But she wasn't so keen on my car-a.

FAST PRINT

www.fastprintreprographics.co.uk

REPROGRAPHICS
PHOTOCOPYING
COLLATION
DYELINE PRINTS
DIGITAL PRINTING

Job no.: 00732

Client: JAY CARTWRIGHT

Job title: SIMON'S CRAP DIARY

500 COPIES B/W
Paid cash.

Signature: Date: 17/10

PEFC
PEFC/10-31-714
Promoting sustainable
forest management
www.pefc.org

TOLLIT & HARVEY LTD.
www.tollitandharvey.co.uk

Europa A5 Notemaker
Lemon
Ref. 3096Z

5 016196 030962 >

Simon's Diary

Parents <u>Do NOT READ</u> this!

Please fuck off

 **EUROPA**® *Notemaker*

A5 feint ruled microperfed - 120 pages

Mix CD plan to make
Carli realise she loves me

The Plan

Show Carli how much I love her - how much I've always loved her - and how it's so right that we're together at last. Also make her realise that I've got a cool taste in music but can be pretty deep too.

Front cover Artwork

Picture of me?
maybe the one from the family holiday to Normandy where I had my shirt off and the shadows make it look like I have a six pack?
   Actually, maybe that's a bit too much. Plus I want her to like me for who I am, not just for my Body.

Picture of Carli?

Could copy one of her Facebook account photos. Could come across as a bit too stalkery?

Sketch of Carli? PERFECT!

A subtle way of showing her my sensitive AND artistic sides.
Could embellish the sketch with some hearts — a way to subliminally reinforce our blossoming relationship and stuff.

Tracks to celebrate
us going out

I kissed a Girl — McFly
Bit literal but it's a good song — and actually the McFly version is way better than the Katie Perry one. Plus, if it's a girl singing it becomes about lesbians which is not how I think of Carli at all. Well, it is
sometimes.

but not right now – now that we're going out.

Are you Gonna Be My Girl – Jet
This is sort of ironic because she already is my girl now. But the lyrics are spot-apart from the bit where the girl in the song is with another man. Actually, what if Carli thinks I think she's with Tom? Or BACK with Tom? Ha! As if that's ever going to happen now...

Everything I Do – Bryan Adams
Because it actually is true. Everything I do is for Carli, and when she hears she'll realise that. Ok, not absolutely everything. Like when I was getting a hand job from Hannah Fields – that wasn't for Carli. Or when I take a shit. But I'd still say 97% of the stuff I do is for Carli. Which is what Bryan Adams meant.

Going Out – Supergrass
Jay got me into supergrass – and this is a classic. I think it's actually about just going for a night out, but Carli will know I actually mean WE'RE going out. Although

We are going for a night out too - at the Fox & Hounds tomorrow after everyone's last exam. First date!?

~~Me so Horny - 2 Live Crew~~
Risky choice. There's a chance it might make her horny about me, or not horny but just thinking it's a hilarious saucy joke. But if she didn't either get horny or laugh, then it could ruin things forever. Best leave it for the next mix CD.

~~Milkshake - Kelis~~
Although I feel like I'd like like to get a milkshake off Carli, I'm actually not 100% sure what a milkshake is. Hand job? Blow job? Probably best I just leave this off the CD - i a milkshake is actually something quite dirty shit, maybe it's a tit wank? - then this track selection is a little bit too full on.

You and Me Song - Wannadies
Carli and me, always - and forever! This one's great for a party - but also has a serious side too.

Which is exactly like me. And Carli too — which is exactly why we make such a great couple. Still can't believe she kissed me. Two kisses really becaused she paused in the middle.

Patience - Take That

Good one to end on because it sends out the message that I don't want to rush things — I'm happy to wait for sex. Well, not "happy" - but I will if she wants to. Plus this was amazing live and when I tell her that and she hears it again she'll think of me - and it still gets played a LOT. Which is good it should because it's an amazing song. Just like Carli's an amazing girl. My amazing girl.

CHRISTMAS PROM THANK YOU SPEECH

By WILLIAM MCKENZIE

Friends, Romans, countrymen

Like Julius Caesar I stand here proud to have served you, my people, to the best of my abilities. I am overjoyed / satisfied / disappointed [delete as appropriate] to see you are all having / not having / had [delete as appropriate] a spectacularly terrible / good [delete as appropriate] time and at this point in the evening's proceedings it behoves me, as chairman elect of the organising committee, to offer a few words of gratitude.

Firstly, I think we can all agree that tonight has been a truly memorable night.

> *[Pause. Make eye contact. Keep chin high. Wait for applause to subside.]*

And while it has been my honour to lead you all on this incredible adventure, I must raise the question; what is a chairman without his committee? What can one man achieve alone? Well, actually quite a lot – I did about 80% of the prom organisation – but it is still right and proper that I should thank the people who did the other 20% (15% being honest). So please show your appreciation for the man who came up with the idea of serving burgers tonight: John!

> *[Open handed gesture to Big John. Move on with speech before the silence becomes too awkward]*

Sterling work, John.

Now while it would have made things technically much simpler to just play a compilation CD over the hall's sound system, I should nevertheless be grateful to tonight's disc jockey, Jay Cartwright!

[Open handed gesture to Jay. Be prepared to cover over any profanity which may either come from Jay, or be directed at him.]

You played some real toe-tappers tonight, so thank you Jay.

Now to the staff.

Miss. Timbs – thank you for your excellent chaperoning, without which the PTA would never have allowed this event to take place. And congratulations also on a term of excellent biology teaching, which in a school such as this is quite an accomplishment.

[Open handed gesture to Miss Timbs – intimately mouth the words "Thank You"]

Then there's ~~Phil Gilbert~~, the head of sixth-form. Mr Gilbert

[Don't pause, just keep things moving]

And finally there's Simon, Neil and Jay – again – who are the closest things I have to friends in this hopefully fleeting phase of my adolescence, so I suppose I ought to thank them too.

Now before you all head off to the bar to use your second and final drinks voucher, may I just add that it hasn't all been plain-sailing and I do have a number of recommendations that next year's chairman would do very well to implement. Should anyone who's thinking of running for office next year wish to discuss them further with me, I'll be over there in the corner of the hall, away from these aurally damaging speakers.

Now eat, drink and be merry! And remember – no more than one burger each!

[Pause. Wait for applause to subside. Stride off-stage purposefully, shaking hands.]

WILL FACE

Rudge Park Comprehensive –
Prom Committee Meeting #001

Facilitator: **Will McKenzie**

Timekeeper: **Will McKenzie**

Note-taker: **Will McKenzie**

Prom Committee Chairman: **Will McKenzie**

Other attendees:
Cooper, S.; Sutherland, N., Cartwright, J.; John, Big; the spotty one (David?);
three girls. *+ quiet little mousey one — who is he?*

—1) Welcome
Aim: Welcome everybody
and impress upon them
the value of teamwork and
exceptional leadership.
TIME LIMIT: No more than
50 seconds
NEXT STEPS: Move on to item ⓪.

0) The Agenda
AIM: Bring everyone's attention to the agenda.
TIMELIMIT: 20—23 seconds
NEXT STEPS: move onto the agenda proper

1) Venue ←

AIM: Get everyone to come to the conclusion that it's happening in the school
hall. There's frankly nowhere else suitable.

TIME LIMIT: 11 seconds.

NEXT STEPS: Research UK law regarding provision of proper signage; I have
serious misgivings regarding the ability of tipsy adolescents to locate the
toilets given the current lack of visual cues.

2) Band

AIM: Get everyone to agree to Transformer playing. I've already booked them (they may be called Transformer Transformer. Or just Transformer. Or Transformer Transformer. I don't know).

TIME LIMIT: 10 seconds.

NEXT STEPS: Convince Jay not to disc jockey and instead let the band play the whole event. Having paid for their services, we should be determined to wring out every last penny of our fee from them.

3) DJ (as distinct from the band)

AIM: See 'next steps' under Item 2 (above)

TIME LIMIT: Assuming Jay doesn't turn up, 6 seconds. If Jay is there, this could quickly descend into a lengthy tit-for-tat argument and last for a good four or five minutes. Stand firm and be bold! Every moment that Jay interjects is a moment we could be discussing my chairman's rights.

NEXT STEPS: Flippantly suggest Jay attends some form of therapy and move on.

4) Food

AIM: Discuss the many and varied options which present themselves when one is catering a large event such as this. Canapés? Fruit? Cheese plate?

TIME LIMIT: 1 minute 45 seconds.

NEXT STEPS: At all costs, prevent Big John from describing the best meals he's ever tasted at the school cafeteria.

5) Chairman's rights

AIM: Surreptitiously obtain the committee's unanimous approval to hand over all authority and decision-making power to me by breezily brushing past this point on the agenda. Also, I alone must have the power to elect next year's Prom Chairman – or, in the (very likely) event that no one of sufficient calibre applies for the post, simply vote myself in for a second term.

TIME LIMIT: As close to zero as I can possibly make it. Minimise time for questions.

NEXT STEPS: Prime minster? Probably some form of ministerial post at the very least.

27) Decoration

AIM: Who's going to decorate the hall? And what will it look like? I don't know. Ask the girls. And also Simon.

TIME LIMIT: Difficult one. I think this could take 10 minutes, especially as I have 8 minutes of my own decorative ideas to discuss. However, if I say 10 minutes, I fear that it may appear as though I'm perpetuating the stereotype that girls talk a lot. I think I just won't mention the intended time limit at the start of this agenda point, and just pray that no one spots the structural anomaly.

NEXT STEPS: Commission a series of photo-montages and detailed CAD drawings of the proposed layout before the school's architect commences work on a 1/100 scale model. See Gilbert re. additional funds required for these most essential of tasks.

28) Clean up

AIM: Decide who's cleaning up the next day, because it sure as hell isn't going to be me. I'm the chairman for God's sake! It'll probably end up being Simon.

TIME LIMIT: Depends how much Si whinges. 4 minutes?

NEXT STEPS: Get him some bin-liners and a mop. And some spermicidal spray. God knows what sort of puddles he'll be cleaning up.

---

29) Undesirables

AIM: Bullying has sadly become rife in Rudge Park, more or less since my arrival and I'd like to use this opportunity to discuss with my committee ways and means of excluding certain undesirable elements of the school community from attending. Donovan. I'm talking about Mark Donovan.

TIME LIMIT: As long as it bloody well takes. I don't want him coming.

NEXT STEPS: Tell Mark Donovan he's not coming. Although, on this occasion, I would be happy to consider delegating this task to Mr. Gilbert.

---

30) AOB

AIM: Not really sure what AOB stands for but it was on the agenda when I downloaded it from the Internet and looks important.

TIME LIMIT: ?

---

31) -

AIM: This point on the agenda left deliberately blank to discuss any other business that may arise.
TIME LIMIT: May the lively debate and learned discussion go on well into the night! Or, at least, eat into a bit of double sociology.

DESCRIBE ONE ACTIONABLE SUGGESTION WHICH WILL IMPROVE THE NEXT MEETING:

MOVE SCHOOLS AGAIN?
KILL THEM?
KILL MYSELF?

Rudge Park Comprehensive School

www.rudgeparkschool.ac.uk

Head teacher: Mr L. Hopkins MA B.Ed

MINUTES OF WEEKLY STAFF MEETING HELD AT 8:00AM ON FRIDAY JANUARY 16th

Present:
Mr. L. Hopkins, Head Teacher
Mr. P. Gilbert, Head of Sixth
Miss. S. Timbs, Biology, Form
Mr. J. Kennedy, Geography
Mr. R. Strawson, Science
Mrs. A. Soper, English
Mr. R. Hoffman, History
Miss. S. Boyce, School Secretary

1. APOLOGIES
No apologies received, although it was noted that Mr. Kennedy arrived late and was not present for points 1 and 2 on the agenda.

2. SECRETARY'S MINUTES
The minutes of last week's meeting were silently approved.

3. HEAD TEACHER'S NOTICES

Disco
Mr. Hopkins reported that the end of term Christmas disco passed largely without incident, although a used prophylactic was discovered in a cleaner's cupboard beside the hall. Facilities manager to be informed and steps taken to encourage the use of locks.

Inspections
With OFSTED inspections due this term, Mr. Hopkins expressed an interest in increasing the number of pupils engaged in extra curricular activities. Mr. Kennedy promptly volunteered to establish a class for 1-on-1 Male Swimming Tuition; those present unanimously voted against.

Smell

Over the Christmas break, the source of the unpleasant smell in the library has been located and eliminated. Uncooked prawns had somehow found their way into several textbooks and storage heaters. Reparations have now been made and the librarian requested to be more vigilant re. shellfish. Mr. Kennedy volunteered to personally interrogate the school's male pupils; Mr. Hopkins declined the offer.

Sport

Without a member of the PhysEd department present, no report was available. Mr. Kennedy requested additional funding for his Greco-Roman wrestling club, so that he could purchase massage oil which would reduce bodily chafing; Mr. Gilbert responded by loudly requesting Mr Kennedy "quieten down, John". No further discussion on the matter.

Excursions

With both the geography & sociology field trip to Swanage and the history field trip to the roman spa at Bath imminent, Mr. Hopkins reported uptake for both had been encouraging although some monies are still outstanding. Mr. Kennedy voiced regret at being unable to attend both trips simultaneously, despite Mr. Hoffman's clarification that he has no connection to the history department. Mr. Hopkins then suggested that it would be valuable if Mr. Gilbert attended the Swanage trip to assist Mr. Kennedy.

Staff Shortages

A number of supply teachers will be present this term to cover illnesses in the mathematics department and maternity leave in the drama department. Mr. Kennedy proposed that he cover the latter and laid out an ambitious plan to get the students to put on a stage version of the film *Brokeback Mountain*, with Mr. Kennedy himself playing one of the leads alongside sixth-former Neil Sutherland. Those present voted unanimously against.

4. ANY OTHER BUSINESS

Miscellaneous ideas were put forth by Mr. Kennedy including the creation of a sports hall changing-room monitor role, making swimming lessons compulsory for years 10 and 11, and a new design for the school football kit along the lines of modern tighter-fitting rugby shirts. With little apparent enthusiasm in the room to pursue these ideas further, the meeting was brought to a close by Mr. Hopkins simply gathering his papers and walking out.

I'm wicked as the robot.

UCAS

Personal statement worksheet

Student Name NEIL SUTHERLAND

This section if for your personal statement. Give evidence of the skills you have that are required to study your chosen subject or attain your elected occupation and how you intend to use the knowledge and experience you will gain. Take care to include details of hobbies, interests and any positions of responsibility held and make specific reference to any relevant jobs, placements or work experience undertaken. 4,000 characters max.

Your course

Why are you applying for your chosen course(s)?

DEAR MR WARWICK UNIVERSITY,

ALRIGHT MATE! I'm ~~Neill~~ Neil and I just wanted to let you know that I think I'm going to come to your uni now.

I WASN'T REALLY SURE before BECAUSE ~~I ENJOYED IT~~ I THOUGHT UNI was all boring and you had to read books and stuff. but I now I've changed my MIND ~~BECAUSE~~ I FOUND OUT it's actually about drinking games and because ~~snag hungry~~ birds go there.

Why does this course interest you? Include eveidence that you understand what's required to study the course.

Only thing is, right, I want to be an airplane driver and I couldn't see airplane ~~driver~~ driving on THE LIST OF SUBJECTS you can DO AT WARWICK. BUT DONT WORRY, cos then I thought "what's an airplane made of?". WELL I DONT ACTUALLY KNOW BECAUSE I'VE never really been near one but I think they're made of a sort of metal. which is sort of chemical. ISN'T IT? And chemicals are to do with chemistry, so I'm going to pick CHEMISTRY. So I can be an airplane driver. Plus chemistry sounds like well good fun. I crave it up at RUDGE Park when I was 14, so it'll be wicked to have another go at doing it again. ②

Why do you think you're suitable for the course(s)?

Oh yeah! I'm supposed to tell you ~~what~~ why I'm well good and that, aren't I? WELL, I once drank a four ~~litre~~ litre ~~bottle~~ bottle of orangeade with all fags butts in it. If my MENTAL MATHEREMETIC SERVES me CORRECTLY, that's like SIXTY PINTS. BUT that is just one of the skills I have which will probably be pretty handy when driving airplanes.

I've also completed Lego Batman on the DS LITE. I've done a two-minute non-stop piss. Two-minutes! I've watched all of Tina Tequila's films which proves I'm dedicated as ~~they're~~ THEY'RE SHIT. and also that I have good ~~knob~~ stamina. ALSO, WHEN I worked on the cheese counter at

Skills and achievements

Universities like to know the skills you have that will help you on the course, or generally with life at university, like any accredited or non-accredited achievements.

→ ASDA I had to work the electric Scaler, which is probably basically the same as what airplane drivers use.

RIGHT, my hands well hurting now because this is the most I've EVER WRITTEN, so I'm going to stop WRITING.

Rudge Park Comprehensive School

Student end of year report: Deputy Head's assessment

Student name: NEIL SUTHERLAND   Year: 6th Form

In many ways, Neil is a dream pupil. Obviously not in an academic sense, but in the sense that he never causes me any trouble. In fact, as Neil's seven year stint at Rudge Park enters its final act, I'm genuinely at a loss to name a single thing Sutherland has done while he's been here. Which means he is precisely the kind of pupil I love having in the sixth form.

With regard to his life beyond this school, well good luck. I am extremely confident that Sutherland will never fulfill his only stated career ambition - airplane driver - but as long as Ryanair exists I guess there is a glimmer of hope.

I suspect that in the spirit of disclosure I am duty bound to state that on one occasion Sutherland did attempt to seek my counsel on a personal matter. An extremely, some might say disturbingly, personal matter. Suffice to say that as the offence he was confessing to occurred outside of school time and seeing as I'm an employee of the state and not a priest, I fell back on my teacher training and got him out of my office before any form filling was required.

I can only conclude that nature must have rectified one of its potentially biggest mistakes because Sutherland never returned to me and the fish counter staff at Asda seem to have stuck with the same line up of late forty-something women for well over nine months now.

Signature: P. Gilbert

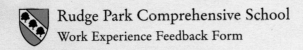

Rudge Park Comprehensive School
Work Experience Feedback Form

Student name: Neil Sutherland

Company: Surrey Chronicle

What were the student's strengths?

Neil showed a great interest in the daily work schedule at a newspaper, with a focus on when lunch occurred and how much time was dedicated to said activity. Neil was also very punctual. He frequently arrived on time and always left on time, or when asked to. He has been an easy student to mentor.

What were the student's weaknesses?

There were a few industry terms I was surprised to find Neil was unfamiliar with, such as "journalist", "paragraph" and "punctuation". But by the end of the two-week placement he understood nearly half of these terms and, I sense, was really starting to get to grips with what a newspaper is.

What are the student's areas for improvement?

My advice to any budding journalist is to read lots and lots of newspapers. In Neil's case, I'd take a step back and say try reading one newspaper. Or, more broadly, any sort of printed material. Anything at all. Perhaps start him on flashcards.

Name and position for the organisation:

Toby Kenny Chief Editor

Form: WEL6001 front

What did you enjoy about your placement?

Well, for my WORK EXPIRIENCE placing I REALLY WANTED to do AIRPLANE DRIVER but they SAID you can't do work EXPIRIENCE on that which is FAIRPLAY I suppose SO I SAID MECHANIC COS I LIKE TEA and nudey calendars. Imagine my SURPRISE WHEN I TURNED up AT the mechanics SHOP only to FIND IT had been turned INTO A NEWSpaper OFFICE. I had BEEN Told before I went this would happen but you CAN STILL

What didn't you enjoy about your placement?

be surprised BY SOMETHING you know is going to happen. WELL I CAN. Anyway I MET the head bloke that runs the NEWSPAPER and decided what goes INTO IT. (DON'T KNOW what he's called) and the head bloke that runs the NEWSPAPER ~~said~~ and decides WHAT GOES IN IT said to go on my lunch break. PRETTY SWEET start. The next week was pretty much the

What did you learn from your work experience?

Same thing. I brung my DS lite in the second day cos they said I could and normally I was Home Just After lunch. Even when I was there I would just sit in the corner keeping my head Down and my nose clean. Just Being quiet and keeping out the way I suppose. Didn't get much

Has your work experience aided your career choices?

to do so it WAS PRETTY sweet Although one afternoon they LET ME SMASH UP some old desks in the SKIP which I had no idea was something NEWSPAPER makers did. So I learned loads about NEWSPAPER making and also about lego Batman on the DS lite. You can use these things called Grapple ~~——~~ Pads and if you press the Y button when

Signature of student:

you are doing double jump on lego batman on the DS lite you can do a double

Form: WEL6001 back

Jump Attack! and at the END of level 7 of lego batman on the DS lite, if you want to defEat CLAY FaCE you have to switch the SPRINKLER ON. So WORK EXPIRIENCE was well useful and the head bloke that RUNS the NEWSPAPER and decides what Goes IN IT Said I was the Best WORK EXPIRIENCE person they Had EVER Had So now I've decided INSTEAD of just being an airplane DRIVER right, I want to be a newspaper person up til LUNCHtimes then I'll be a Airplane driver in the Afternoons.

GORD CORONET POO

DVD Reviews

This week, our DVD reviews have been written by Neil Sutherland, a young news hound who has been on work experience from Rudge Park Comprehensive.

Cert. 12

The Social Network

The worst film ever. Don't go and see it. All the people spoke like a million words a minute which is well hard to follow. The main bloke's hair was shit. Barely any fit birds in it. Too long, too bent. It's not even about the best bits of Facebook, like looking at pics of girls you fancy, or girls you don't fancy but in their bikinis, joining funny groups which is a right laff, or spaffing one out over Will's mum's profile pic.

Cert. 12

Inception

What the fuck was that all about? My head hurts. It looked well cool and that, but I have literally no idea what just happened. It might as well have been in Chinese. The bloke that runs the paper reck-

oned it was made by the bloke that made *The Dark Knight*. Thanks mate, I sat through two and a half hours of this headache waiting for Batman to appear. He doesn't. My head still hurts.

Cert. 15

Sex and the City 2

That is two hours of my life I ain't getting back. It started well, the title was sexy, but after that it went downhill fast. Yes it has got some sex in it, but it's always one of these four well old birds doing it and you barely see any nips. They should have called it some grannies that never shut up who occasionally have boring sex in the city. Not good.

Cert. G

Shrek Forever After

On the box for this one, it said there was some well famous

people in this like Cameron Diaz and Eddie Murphy. But I couldn't see them for the first hour of the film, until I realised the actors and actoresses were wearing, like, costumes and make-up so they didn't look like they do normally.

Cert. 18

Piranha 3D

Fuck *Avatar*, this is what 3D was invented for... Kelly Brook's norks coming right at you. It felt like I could get one in my mouth. I couldn't, no matter how hard I tried, but that was my only complaint. Killer fish and Kelly Brook, this might be the best film ever made. I bet it cleans up at the Oscars.

Cert. PG

The Last Airbender

Honest to God, the funniest film I've ever seen. Up to now, my number one comedy film was *Big Momma's House 2*, but now it's this by a mile. That's because there's like this catchphrase they all do, all the time in the film where they keep calling each other benders. They're like "You're a bender!" and then the other one will be like "You're going to be the greatest bender ever. Let's go get the other benders." And it just keeps going. Genius! But it's not just really really really funny, the story is good too. It's about these kind of wizards who can bend stuff like water, which is amazing because I didn't even think you could actually scientifically bend water.

Cert. PG

Legends Of The Guardians: The Owls Of Ga'Hoole

Being totally up front about this, I spilt my can of Relentless on the DVD case, and it got inside the DVD case and made the DVD all sticky. Tried it in the DVD player just in case it worked, but no, it didn't work. Looking at the picture on the box though, if you're into magical owl movies, then this could probably be a good one.

Text and photos by Neil Sutherland

Student name: Neil Sutherland

Brief idea: <u>To get loads of money out of fruit machines.</u> I love fruities. They're like big computer games what give you money and it's the law that every pub in the world has to have at least one in, usually near the girls' toilets. I like them because they're way more interesting than people, they never ask you for ID and the best bit is that unlike gambling, it's actually IMPOSSIBLE to get addicted to them. I could well easily stop playing fruit machines if I wanted to. Thing about them is though they're not as easy as they look. Unless you're an expert like me. First of all, there isn't any fruit ANYWHERE inside. They're not made of fruit and you can't win fruit out of them – only money. Took me a few goes to realise that.

But once you've got your head around the fruit / no fruit thing, there's loads of ways to get money out of them. So I'm going to be nice and share my fruitie strategies with you all so you can get rich like me.

WATER COINS

I came up with that one. It's where you press some pound coins into Blu-Tack (why do they call it that? mental) to make like a mould. Then you fill the mould holes with water and put it all in the freezer. Then, wallop – pound coin shaped ice cubes! They're the same size as real ones and they weigh the same too, so the fruitie doesn't know the difference. Thing is though this only really works in winter. And in a really cold pub that's really close to your freezer. And you have to carry a cool bag which does look a bit weird. Also, don't put too many in or the fruit machine starts fizzing, stops working and then all the lights in the pub go off and then you deffo can't get any money out. But also, don't put a load of water coins in your pocket and then forget you did or you'll end up looking like you pissed yourself. Trust me, it's well embarrassing.

   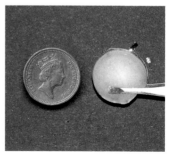

GUM COINS

This one's a bit like water coins but doesn't involve water. Or Blu-Tack. Or a freezer. But it does involve coins. What you do is get two 10 peso coins from Mexicoland and then stick them together with a bit of chewie. Or you could use Blu-Tack. As far as the Deal or No Deal fruitie in the Black Bull's concerned, two 10 peso coins stuck together look exactly like a pound coin when they're actually worth, like, 2p or something. I got a load of Mexicolandish coins from my uncle Gary who was in prison there for a bit, but it's probably not worth driving there to get your own as the petrol will cost loads.

THE HAMMER

"The hammer" is where you hit all the buttons at once in the hope that it will make a hidden game happen. It never really works. Although I did see a guy down the Bull do a hammer so hard that it dislodged something inside and a bit of plastic came out of the coin slot. He got asked to leave, but he got to keep the plastic bit, so he was quids in.

THE SLAP

"The slap" is a bit like the hammer but instead of hitting all the buttons, you just hit the side of the fruitie instead. My uncle Gary says it used to work with tellys and girls in the 70s, although I don't really know what he means because you can't win money from TVs or girls from the 70s.

OTHER IDEA

The other idea I've had is about getting a job at the factory where they make the fruit machines in the first place. If you worked there long enough, you'd eventually become, like, the manager which means you'd know everything there is to know about how it all works – all the bonus rounds, all the nudge sequences and the cash game prize runs. And you could probably build in like a secret button that automatically paid out jackpot. Then you could go into any pub with your quiz machine in and win like a thousand pounds. It probably takes years to get to manager though so I'm not sure it's worth it.

SECRET IDEAS

I've obviously got loads more fruitie strategies but I don't want to give them away and also I've only ever really played on the Deal or No Deal fruit machine in the Black Bull. But it's only a matter of time before I go pro and there's easily a book in all this, so if anyone who makes books for a living is reading this and wants to pay me loads to write the book then I'd probably consider definitely doing it. Cheers.

HOLD THE BELLS

Oh yeah, one more. Always, always hold the bells. But then everyone knows this one already.

From: shuttlecockkevin12@hotmail.co.uk
To: Christmas group
Date: 20th December 2009 at 11:30
Subject: Merry Christmas!

Dear friends and family,

I hope you'll forgive this one-size-fits-all round robin letter to update you on all things Sutherland from this past year, but I'm so busy with work that there simply isn't enough time to write individual letters to you all. More's the pity!

So, onto our news. Neil is in his final year at Rudge Park and apparently doing well. In fact, at parent(s) evening Mr. Kennedy, who I presume to be his P.E. teacher, informed me he was not only a very open-minded boy but also that he has an excellent physique. Outside of school, Neil has been working at our local ASDA supermarket store and has struck up some solid friendships with his colleagues. I'm so proud of what a sociable boy he has become; his experiences on the cheese counter signify how capable he is of bonding with people of any age. For those of you who were at Neil's 18th birthday, thank you for coming and I hope you enjoyed the first couple of hours (before things went awry).

Katie is still living at home while she continues her crusade to get her manicured foot in the door of the modelling industry. Or singing industry. Or TV presenting industry. I have suggested to her that she might also like to consider a career in youth work, because she has a wonderful rapport with teenagers; Neil's friends for example hang on her every word. But Neil and I obviously are very glad that she's sticking around – the last thing we want is another female flying the nest! Touch of gallows humour there.

Now for me. As usual there hasn't been an awful lot of time for socialising. The children tend to monopolise most of my energy and what's left of me I try and save for the badminton club guys. However I did recently spend a delightful afternoon with a young divorcee named Polly. Despite our differences we found we had much in common – well, teenage sons with issues about their work experience placements and unfaithful former partners. Polly was incredibly empathetic to my plight (as a fellow single parent) and kept reiterating how there was absolutely nothing wrong with it these days and that I shouldn't let other people's prejudice stop me from being who I am. Such an inspirational lady. Alas, I didn't seize the chance to formally arrange another date but Polly has since enquired if I had any plans for watching the upcoming Eurovision Song Contest, so watch this space.

Finally, as in previous years, we've barely seen Neil and Katie's ~~Jezebel~~ mother.

Merry Christmas and a Happy New Year to you all!

Kevin Sutherland

Rudge Park Comprehensive School
Biology Coursework on Reproduction part 1

Candidate number: [   ]

Student name: Neil Sutherland

Abstract: do you put the balls in

Introduction:

So the reason I am writing about this is because there is some PEOPLE WHO Think that during sensual INTERCOURSE men just put the penis into the ladys vag (diagram 1) but then there are some people who think that ~~thing~~ you also put the balls in aswell (diagram 2)

i know it sounds a bit mucky for school work but if you THINK ABOUT it without reproduction there wouldn't be any more PEOPLE. so TALKING ABOUT whether THE NADS GO IN the fanny is actually very serious for THE SURVIVAL of the HUMAN RACE.

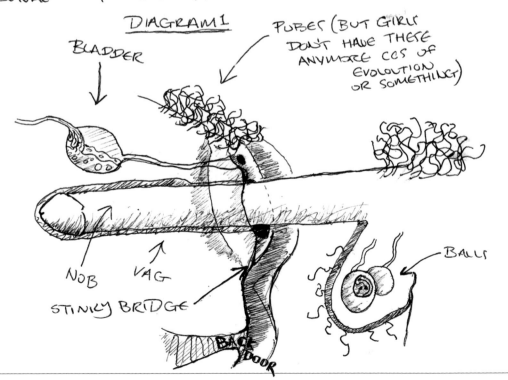

DIAGRAM 1

BLADDER

PUBES (BUT GIRLS DON'T HAVE THESE ANYMORE COS OF EVOLUTION OR SOMETHING)

NOB

VAG

STINKY BRIDGE

BACK DOOR

BALLS

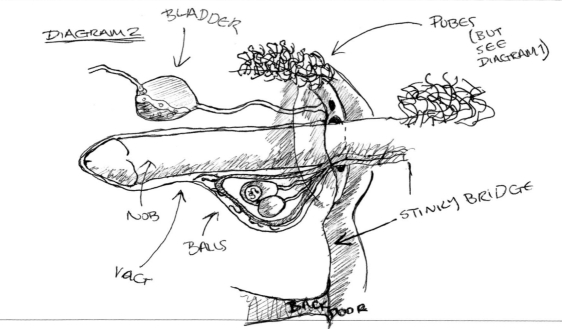

DIAGRAM 2

BLADDER

PUBES (BUT SEE DIAGRAM 1)

STINKY BRIDGE

NOB

BALLS

VAG

BACK DOOR

Method:

So THE first way I thought of finding JUT The answer was to ask ~~10 girls~~ birds to have Sensual intercourse with me. THEN I would GO TO put my balls in and just watch to SEE if they reckoned that WAS NORMAL. If 6 ~~say~~ birds didn't make a big deal out of it then obviously you DO put the BALLS in. I'd then PRESENT my results in a table like this:

table 1 - results of INTRODUCING THE BALLS INTO 10 GIRLS *

	BIRD NUMBER/NAME	MADE A FUSS AFTER PODS PUSHED IN
1	Fitty	N
2	AVERAGE	N
3	BUFF	N
4	Hot	Y
5	mutter	N
6	ugly but dirty	Y
7	will's mum	Y
8	Slutty	N
9	Nuts model	N
10	The twins	N

In the above example seven girls or something didn't seem to think it was weird so that would prove you do put the balls in. but like I say that was my first thought for AN EXPERIMENT AND WHEN we was checking our experiments with miss timbs she said that wasn't REALLY OK for lots of ethnical reasons WHICH IS A FAIR POINT I s'pose. So INSTEAD I just did two simple methods; I asked a SEX EXPERT and looked it up on THE INTERNET.

Results:

the SEX EXPERT[1] I spoke to said you deffo put the balls in. HE SAID THAT FIRST you GET A STIFFY then you put that in then you slip in the left bollock followed by the right bollock. PROBLEM is if you don't put the BALLS in the sperm GET lost ALONG the way into the fanny cos there only small[2] but if the Gonads are already in the fanny then they CANT GET LOST. SIMPLES. also THEY LOVE it, the more up there the BETTER. Always.

onto my other method. I DID research on the topic on my dads laptop. there were already one or two useful pages STORED IN HIS HISTORY but I went to lots of different SITES to make sure NO one was TRICKING me Again and observed all the Gonads very closely which is not SOMETHING I USUALLY DO but miss TIMBS says it's good to do things you don't normally do cos that makes you smarter. there was even something on wikipedia about it but I Got a bit sidetracked AND ENDED UP DOING SOMETHING Totally different.

So basically, i still Don't know if you put the balls in or not. the only thing that I can say is 100% true is that if you don't put them in the girl deffo can't get pregnant.

Discussion:

If that I was going to do this EXPERIMENT again which I will because I'm leaving school and won't ever WANT TO DO homework again I would probably just go back to my plan of intercoursing 10 girls because the internet's way to confusing.

that's the end of my Report. this is Niel Sutherland, Rudge Park Comprehensive School. Cheers. Goodnight.

Footnotes

1. the sex expert i refer to is JAY CARTWRIGHT who has an open UNIVERSITY sex degree.

2. SPERMS ARE about the size of Tadpoles.

*These results are made up. I Don't really know How 10 girls would react. to be honest I DON'T really know TEN GIRLS so I had to make it up for the sake of the TEST.

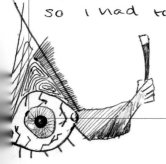

0/10 See me please

NICE! course miss RESULT

GEOGRAPHY AND SOCIOLOGY FIELD TRIP TO SWANAGE
PUBLIC TRANSPORT SURVEY

BY *Jay Cartwright* (23) NEIL SUTHERLAND

Opening lines to say to fit MILFs:
"Excuse me, we're doing a survey for school. Can I ask you a few questions?"

1) What form of transport did you take into town today?

Drove Car

2) How often do you use public transport?

☐ 1 ☐ 2 ☐ 3 ☐ 4 ☐ 5   Rarely

3) Do you wear stockings and that?

☐ 1 ☐ 2 ☐ 3 ☐ 4 ☐ 5   Unsure

At this point the MILF refused to answer any more questions. Must be Frigid. As such, Neil and I have estimated her responses

4) Do you enjoy anal?

☐ 1 ☐ 2 ☐ 3 ☐ 4 ☐ 5

From this point forward. By the look of her I reckon she well-loved anal.

5) Would you use public transport more if buses were more regular?

☐ 1 ☐ 2 ☐ 3 ☐ 4 ☐ 5   I bet she gets ridden more than a bus anyway

6) If you met a lad in this precinct who you got all horny for, how far would you let him go with you on that same afternoon?
a) Two fingers
b) Spaff on tits
c) Angry dragon
d) All of the above ✓ Clearly dripping for it.

7) Do you think there are enough cycle lanes in Swanage?

☐ yes ☐ no   I bet she gets ridden more than a bike anyway.

8) The answer to the next question will be recorded onto the voice recorder on my phone so that it can be analysed at a later date. What is your muckiest sexual fantasy?
By the looks of it, probably involves a cup and two girls.

9) How many times, on average, do you cycle into the town centre a week?

Probably about 50 — she looks like the town bike

10) How many lesbian experiences have you had?
a) 1 to 5
b) 6 to 10
c) 11 to 100
d) So many I've lost count. ✓ *without a doubt.*

11) Do you think Swanage would benefit from a public transport interchange?

☐ yes ☐ no *I think she'd benefit from my cock in her interchange.*

12) In reference to question 10, please describe all the lesbian experiences you have had.

See answer to question 8.

13) How frequently do you use the Swanage Park & Ride service?
a) Daily ✓ *She is the Park + Ride service!*
b) Weekly
c) Monthly
d) Never

14) Which genre of porn do you mostly strum one out to?
a) Girl on girl
b) Gang bangs
c) French girl on girl
d) French girl on girl gang bangs ✓

15) Do you ever use the Swanage night bus service?

☐ yes ☐ no *She doesn't need to. She probably always gets lifts off blokes in exchange for a free blowie.*

16) If you answered "yes" to question 15, have you ever had a shag on the Swanage night bus service?

☑ yes ☐ no *Of course she has.*

17) If you answered "Yes" to question 16, was it in the clunge or the backdoor?

Bound to be double entry.

18) If you answered "backdoor" to question 17, did you love it?

☑ yes ☐ no *Yes.*

19) Please could you provide me with your home address and mobile telephone number in case additional questions arise?

Miss Horny Clittington, 69 Ballsdeep Alley, Swanage Tel. 0909 69 69 69

Closing lines to say to fit MILFs:
"Thank you for taking the time to answer all twenty questions in this survey. Your honest answers have been both informative and arousing."

"Are you the Swanage MILF?"

A TO Z OF SEX

Right Si, it's a good job you've got me and Neil as mates because otherwise your sad little sex trip to Warwick is guaranteed to be a total and utter fucking disaster. There's nothing I don't know about nobbing birds. That's why every year the Oxford English Dictionary ask me to check whether they've missed out any sex words. I normally charge for this, but because I've just had a three-way with the fit girl who works at the BP garage and a lady trucker, I'm in a good mood so here it is for free: the definitive A to Z of sex.

Don't lose it – it's top secret. And probably worth, like, a million quid cos I wrote it. Although Neil's shitty drawings have probably brought the price down a bit. Anyway, these are the absolute basics so you need to know it ALL inside out (just like I do with the garage girl's anal passage).

A is for Anilingus

Birds love to do a bit of rimming. Especially European ones. So much so that anilingus is what French girls call "First Base". But personally speaking, even if it was a real fitty asking for it, you'd never get my tongue near her bumhole.

B is for ~~Bumming~~ ~~Boners~~ ~~Badminton~~ ~~Bi-curious~~ ~~Bumders~~ ~~Ballsack~~

Nah, can't think of a B.

C is for Chute Job

That's getting a blowie on a waterslide. Copyright Jay Cartwright, aged 13, Camber Sands Water Park.

D is for Doggy-style

Position of choice for professional footballers cos it improves core stability, strengthens the knees joints and also means you can use the bird's bangers for balance.

E is for Expert

Which is what I am at sex, ever since I got my fifth dan black johnnie at sex grading in Sweden.

F is for Flaps

One of the three main parts of the minge, along with the hole and the clitty. The clitty's the most important bit though. Some people think it's difficult to find, but that's bollocks. It's slap bang in the middle of the fanny and the arsehole.

G is for Gumjob

It's about making the best of a bad lot when you're fucking anyone over 45, and getting them to remove their false teeth first makes blowies much better.

H is for Hore

Birds who get paid for sex. I get paid for sex though and I'm not a hore. I'm a sex-teacher.

I is for Inside The Clunge

Absolute bare minimum on a first date or the bird's frigid.

J is for Johnnie

Guaranteed hard-on killer, especially if you've got a monster schlong like me. I have to import mine from America cos they don't make them big enough for me in Europe, but even the jumbo yank ones are a bit small on me.

K is for Kissing

Bit boring, but it does get birds all frothed up. The rule is: three kisses, then tits for a bit, then get in there with the finger-bang. The more fingers the better.

L is for Lezzers

Chicks who love munching minge. Even though they're technically only supposed to go for other birds, I'm yet to meet one who didn't want a piece of my fat cock. But then I am exceptional.

M is for MILFF

Mum I'd Love to Finger and Fuck. Like Will's Mum. We'd all like to get knuckle deep before bending her over Will's desk and doing her from behind, wouldn't we?

N is for Nipples

Boring. When you've seen one, you've seen 'em all. And I should know cos I've seen 'em all.

O is for Organ Cheese

What you get if you don't wash your nob for a week. French birds love it.

P is for Pickle Rigger

That's a basic. I know you're a virgin, but even YOU don't need that one explaining to you, do you?

Q is for the Queen

She might be in her 80s or whatever, but I still would. I'd deffo get her to suck my crown jewels.

R is for Red Hot Dutch

Swedish code for sex in a sauna. I did it 8 times a day when I was on holiday there.

S is for Spooje

Spunk. Man sauce. Jizz. Population paste. Or, if your parents are asking what the stain is, spilt yoghurt.

T is for Tactical Wank

Proper athletes warm up before a big race, and sex is no different. I told that to the all-girl squad I coached at the 2010 Sex Olympics and guess what? They got gold in the team gang-bang.

U is for Underwear, knickers and that

Most commonly found on my bedroom floor. Most of the birds I shag have stopped even bothering wearing it now, cos they're so keen to get my length up them. Good way to get past the school's internet controls.

V is for Vaclunginius

The Latin word for Clunge. And probably what Will calls it too.

W is for World Wank Web

What the www stands for in the internet.

X is for Xylophone Sticks

Might not sound sexual at first, but Neil's sister used to let me stick them in her fanny when I was younger.

Y is for Yacht

"What's a yacht got to do with sex, Jay?" I hear you ask. Well, I was on a yacht in Monte Carlo when I had my first orgy, back in the day, when I was 14. The rocking of the boat helped my shagging rhythm. Jizzed on 12 girls in one afternoon. Happy days.

Z is for Zookeeper

Fucked one once. Kinky bitch. Made me do it in the penguin enclosure. I'm telling you, it was like a porn remake of Madagascar. Not cos I had sex with any animals – I only fucked the fit zookeeper. Although the panda had kind eyes.

Rudge Park Comprehensive School
Student end of year report: Deputy Head's assessment

Student name: JAY CARTWRIGHT   Year: 6th form

What Jay Cartwright lacks in academic ambition, he more than makes up for in creativity (a far less valuable quality). Jay has certainly been blessed with a vivid imagination, along with an encylopaedic knowledge of vulgarities. His ability to deliver eye-watering euphemisms is sadly unmatched by his ability to deliver coursework - which has, variously, been "lost over the side of P Diddy's yacht", stolen by the SAS for "breaching public safety" and "fired in a pod towards Uranus, as an illustration of human achievement to aliens". I strongly suspect one, and perhaps more of these, are untrue.

While tutoring Jay hasn't always been easy, we have occasionally discovered some common ground. For example, Jay has made it abundantly clear that he does not believe there is any point in him furthering his education beyond Rudge Park, and I wholeheartedly agree. Back in better times, Cartwright would have been the perfect candidate for a polytechnic course. He would have been able to train in a more practical field leading to a manual job where he would inevitably have the rough edges knocked off him by some no-nonsense working class colleagues. Essentially vocational lessons, followed by some necessarily voilent life lessons.

Signature:

Continuation:

However, now that Thatcher/Major/Blair (take your pick, they all played their part) have slapped some cheap make-up onto polys in a woeful attempt to make them look like actual universities, the likes of Cartwright have nowhere to go. Other than, perhaps, the back of the queue of whichever Saturday night talent show happens to be recruiting deluded freaks at this moment in time.

I understand from his visit to the careers adviser that Cartwright's preferred job is "becoming a brand". Whilst I don't doubt that some ex-poly somewhere will offer a three-year course in this (these days, you could probably do an MA in Breathing at one of those tin pot "Universities"), I feel that perhaps Jay may be better off picking a more realistic career option eg. he's got more chance of ~~being~~ becoming an astronaut. I'm aware that sarcasm is not always communicated clearly in written form, so please let me clarify that my astronaut suggestion was, indeed, highly sarcastic.

But of all the many and varied pupils under my care, I can hand on heart say that Jay Cartwright is the one and only boy with that name. Although I do believe there's a Jay Arkwright in year eleven.

Signature: P. Gilbert

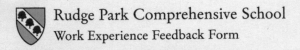

Rudge Park Comprehensive School
Work Experience Feedback Form

Student name: **Jay Cartwright**

Company: **Cartwright Plant Hire (my Dad's firm)**

What were the student's strengths?

The "student" was very strong at standing around and being a useless twat. It was as if he'd had years of practice.

I've just spent half an hour trying to think of something else to write in this section, and I've come up with sweet F.A.

What were the student's weaknesses?

Jay's main responsibility was throwing stuff into a skip. But unfortunately, he was very slow at putting stuff into the skip. Some of the stuff he attempted to put into the skip actually missed the skip, and some of the stuff he did manage to get into the skip wasn't actually meant for the skip. Like tools. And cement.

What are the student's areas for improvement?

He needs to be less lazy, he needs to be able to throw stuff without looking like a girl and he needs to lower his standards with the birds.

Name and position for the organisation:

Terry Cartwright   Owner

Form: WEL6001 front

What did you enjoy about your placement?

I think the best bit was when I was asked to a big important business meeting and I single-handedly negotiated a 30 year, multi-million pound contract for Cartwright's Plant Hire. Made me realise that I would be well good at being a Football agent. Which is great, cos it means that when I leave school and sign pro forms for West Ham, I can sort out my own deal and keep the commission.

What didn't you enjoy about your placement?

Having to throw stuff into skips. And also they didn't have enough materials to make decent ramps with, which meant that I was only able to jump 6 diggers with the digger I was driving. With a proper ramp, I could have jumped 10 diggers easy.

What did you learn from your work experience?

Nothing, it's impossible to learn anything when you have as much experience as me. I s'pose I did learn one thing — my Dad can spend up to two hours a day in a porta loo with the Daily Star.

Has your work experience aided your career choices?

Not really. It made me realise that I'm basically amazing at everything I try which, if anything, makes my career choices even more difficult. Normal people's job decisions are narrowed down by what they can do mentally and physically, but obviously that's not the case for me. I think my ultimate career aim remains unchanged though — to become a brand. I'll make money off my own lines of merchandise like sportswear, aftershave and DJ compilation CDs.

Signature of student:

Jay Cartwright 23

Form: WEL6001 back

SEND To: Peter Jones Dragon, James Caan Dragon, Duncan Bannatyne Dragon, Woman Dragon, Steve Jobs, Beckham, whoever's in charge of NatWest, Avram Grant, Bono, Alan Sugar (and Nick and Margaret and Karen), Richard Branson, everyone who's ever been on Secret Millionaire.

JAY CARTWRIGHT'S BUSINNESS PLAN

THE MAN • THE BRAND • THE LEGEND

THE TOPLINE

We're both busy people so let's cut the shit and get to the point: if you're reading this then you're one of the lucky few I've hand-picked to share my amazing business brain and guaranteed money-making idea with. No bullshit: I am going to be massive, so if you want a slice then here's your chance, but act quick. All I need is one million quid to get my business up and running. After that it's pure profit and I guarantee you'll get 1% of everything I earn in the first year (which will be way more than £1m so you'd have to be a muppet not to give me the cash).

THE IDEA

I've basically got loads of wicked ideas and will probably end up doing them all but the one I reckon it's easiest to get started with is: car stereos. If you think about it, it's genius. What I'll do is offer a personal service to mega-rich clients all over the world to fit well tasty car stereos for them and their WAGS. This is an amazing idea for four reasons:

1) Rich people love listening to music in their car (especially pop stars cos it's their work, isn't it?)
2) Rich people have loads of cars – so they'll need loads of stereos fitted.
3) Rich people can't be bothered to do anything themselves so will happily shell out for someone else (me) to do it for them.
4) Rich people have got so much money, you can stick an extra couple of grand on the bill and they don't even notice.

The reason I'll be so good at it is I know loads about car stereos. I've been writing anonymous reviews of the best audio equipment for Max Power since I was twelve and my grandad invented MP3s, so it's in the blood. For example, I know that Kenwood make the loudest stereos by miles but I'll also fit Sony, Blaupunkt, JVC, and Panasonic – whatever my clients want, really.

If they pay extra I'll even fit a woofer in the parcel shelf and do custom jobs, although those will really cost and I'll probably have to rope in my old mate Xzibit who I taught how to pimp cars.

SatNav's a bit fiddly to fit though so I probably won't bother with that, also everyone's got one now so no money in it

THE CLIENTS

Don't worry. I've got a specific target demographic in mind. I'm not going to waste my time rummaging around under the dashboard of some bloke off Hollyoaks' Seat Ibiza. That's why my target market is: proper Hollywood A-listers. Direct too, not through their agents or any of that bollocks. I've already mentioned bits of my idea (without giving it all away of course) at a couple of Oscar parties and here's what people are already saying about it:

"I got 99 problems – and one of them is the shitty car stereo in my new Lambo. Please sort it out for me Jay?"
– P. Diddy

"I might have made the greatest rock 'n' roll album of all time but it sounds shit out of the speakers that came with my Rolls Royce. Jay, you know loads about car stereos so can you fix it? Cash, yeah?"
– Noel Gallagher

"Jay you stud. I'm, like, totally embarrassed to give you a lift in my new Ferrari cos the stereo doesn't even do Bluetooth and the bass is all flabby. Work some magic on it and you can poke(r) my face xx"
– Lady Gaga

CASHFLOW

I reckon I can make more than £30m in my first year of fitting car stereos and this is how:

I've had a squizz on eBay and you can get a pretty decent-looking car stereo for £30. So I'll use most of the £1m you give me to buy those, although I will need to keep a bit back for a new suit, Tag watch and a Vertu mobile phone because when you're operating in such a high-end market you've got to look the part, as I'm sure you know. So if I take out £5,000 for that, that means I'll still have enough left over to buy 33,166.666 car stereos online – call it 33,166 after I've saved on postage by buying them all at once. The I'll pay Neil £100 per week to fit them and I'll make a £1,000 a go which means I'll make £33,166,000. Minus your 1% – and that makes £33,166,999 profit for me! In under a year! And that's just a guess – could be much more.

WHY YOU SHOULD INVEST

Because I'm Jay Cartwright.

I started selling pick'n'mix to kids at school when I was nine and within a year I was Managing Director, with a company car that I couldn't even drive, turning over £80m. But I lost all that on the stock market crash. I was skint for a bit but things picked up the following year when I met David Beckham at West Ham and told him to go to Galaxy – for a 15% cut. He insisted 20% was fairer so I nutmegged him and took him for peri peri chicken with my two Nandos black cards.

And that's just the tip of the Cartwright iceberg. Because outside my extensive working life, I also have a few hobbies. This might help you see what a well rounded success story I am:

I can do 100 one-arm sit ups in under a minute. When I did under 11s boxing, I beat the shit out of Amir Khan. Three of Banksy's paintings are actually ones I did. I've got an electric thumb. I've passed 15 GCSEs but I did them when I was on Easter holidays in France so they're French ones and they don't count over here. I thrashed Lewis Hamilton to become national karting champion when I was 12. I can eat a phall without drinking anything. I ghost-wrote Russell Brand's autobiography and all the sexual stuff in it is actually things I did. Ben and Jerry's named an ice cream flavour after me called "Cart-Right Chocolatey". I was on the books at West Ham but I packed in football because I didn't like the way the game was going – too commercial, soul's gone out of it. I've visited 100 countries. Paul Weller wanted to adopt me but my Dad started crying so I left it. I once swam the channel for a dare – only took me six hours. I once won the Bellagio in Las Vegas in a game of poker but decided to give it back. Standing on the ground, I smashed a 60th floor window in Canary Wharf with a tennis ball – the police let me off because they were so impressed. I've done enough hours in a helicopter to earn my pilot's license, but I can't be fucked to take the test. I once drew a picture of Big Ben from memory and everyone thought it was an actual photo. The Kings Of Leon had an argument at Glastonbury and stormed off stage, so I got out the crowd and just did some acoustic versions of their songs and got 9/10 in the NME. From a standing start I can jump over a Mini. I got kicked out of Diversity for being too creative with my choreography. West Ham pay me a hundred quid a week to watch matches on Sky Sports and scout new players for them. I've got a prototype 512GB 3D iPod which Apple are getting me to test out – but if I show it to anyone they'll sue me for $60 million, which I could pay, but I won't.

WHAT NEXT?

It's first come, first served I'm afraid so if you want to get involved then you've gotta move quick because I'm anticipating a LOT of interest. Wire me the cash to account number 5526517, sort code 00-99-23, drop me a line on 07700 900518 and we'll take it from there.

Dear Jay

I don't want you to be my valentine, I want you to give it to me hard and all over the shop: up the bum, on a chair, front ways, back ways, two's up, lying down, the lot.

Guess who??

Dear Jay

I've been watching you for a while, and I have no doubt you are packing the biggest cock I've ever seen. But not just that. I can tell from the way you walk that you know exactly what to do with it when you are having sex using it (your massive cock).

A Secret Admirer
who will kill themselves if you don't give it to me in the next seven days (I understand Sundays are out cos of the secret training you give the England Football team).

Dear Jay

Sorry this card is soaking wet, I just got too horny and squirted all over it.

Please be my Valentine, darling?

Dear Jay

I think I love you, and hope that one day you could love me too. I know you want love and someone to talk to, we all do.

Be my Valentine (one day?)

10th September

So I can legally drive a car by myself now. I passed my driving test! Which means no more boring driving lessons and no more evenings of practice with Dad spending the whole time telling me what he got up to with Mum in his first car, only really stopping to ask me to slow down. Which is ridiculous, because I'd probably be fine all the way up to 150 MPH and anyway I always slow down for speed cameras so who bloody cares? Such a dick. What's the point in driving if you can't have any fun? And I'm not talking about the fun which led to Dad's back seat growing mould. RANK.

The test itself was totally uneventful and normal. I just kind of got everything right and so then the examiner passed me. Nothing unusual happened.

When I got home there was good news and bad news. The good news was that I won my bet with Andrew so he had to give me his Nintendo DS. I don't even want it but its the principle isn't it? I'll probably just put it on ebay, though I can't imagine I'd get more than 20 quid for it. Thinking about it, I might be better off if I just sell it back to him for 60 quid. Now the bad news for passing my test, Mum and Dad bought me a car. Sounds good, but the car is a pile of shit. A total fucking embarrassment. It's yellow! Yellow and shit. If I sold it on eBay I'd get less for it than the DS. It's got a bloody tapedeck. YES, that's right. TAPE DECK! It might as well have had a fucking gramophone or a penny farthing. I don't want to be seen near it, let alone driving it. Trust Dad to find the one car which is actually worse than not having a car at all.

This is so typical of my fucking stupid parents. They never think about what I want, what I might actually like. I bet I could get them for child abuse or something. They reckoned that lots of kids would love to get a car for a present and that me calling it shit was being ungrateful. But how can you be ungrateful if you're telling the truth? They just don't see it. It's like they've kicked me in the bollocks and I think I should feel lucky because most other parents don't kick their kids in the bollocks. I often think I'd be better off if they died. My life would be much less annoying, plus I'd get my inheritance while I'm still young enough to enjoy spending it on cool stuff. They're way too old for it now anyway. I know they do come in useful sometimes like when Dad picked me, Will, Jay and Neil up from Thorpe Park car park yesterday evening (because of some car related stuff that wasn't my fault). But then again, if I had their inheritance I could just get cabs everywhere instead. Obviously I don't actually want them dead—not yet, I wouldn't kill them. I'm not a nutter. But if they were going to both die perhaps the best cause of death for all concerned would be if they fatally crashed in my Fiat Hawaii (Provided the car was a total write-off and the insurance company didn't refuse to pay out because it's so shit).

21st September

After comparing notes with Neil Groves in the year above, my driving test was a little bit weird, maybe, actually.

SIMON COOPER'S GUIDE TO

Cocktails

There might not be a lot I know about - other than which clubs to use in golf and what it's like to have world-class morons for parents - but I'd definitely say that cocktails is one of my strengths. You could even call it a hobby because I've been making cocktails for over a year now and have easily made ten different ones. They usually cost a bomb to buy in the pub but they're actually pretty easy to make at home. After all, it's just putting one drink in a cup and then putting another drink in on top. And sometimes putting a third drink in too. Anyway, here are my top ten.

Mean Green

Take some vodka, whisky and crème de menthe and add them all to a bottle. When Will and I did this we used an empty two-litre coke bottle but any bottle will do. Then shake it up loads and that's it really. Sort of tastes like minty whisky but it gets you happy. Don't let it get too warm though or it starts smelling of bleach. And behaving like it too.

Orange Borange

Orangeade and Blue Bols. The name "Orange Borange" is a bit misleading actually because it comes out green (well actually, when it comes out yellow with lumps in, but that's only if you have too much.). But I've already used the name "Mean Green" and couldn't really think of anything else.

Orange Worange

Orangeade and wine. Any wine will do: red, white or the other sort. Neil introduced me to this up in Warwick and it actually tastes better than it sounds. Which isn't hard because it sounds rank.

Orange Wisorange

Orangeade and whisky. Another one of Neil's creations. This one tastes worse than it sounds actually. Probably wouldn't bother with this one actually.

Orange Vorange (copyright Neil Sutherland)

Orangeade and vodka. Much more classy than my other orangeade-based cocktails and more of an after-dinner drink. Only downside is it turns your poo orange.

Sleepy Head

Sleeping pills, Ribena, red wine and cough mixture; all mixed half and half. Adding some Lucozade does something to it but I can't remember what. I haven't actually tried this one – it was Neil's idea mostly.

Beerwine

Some beer with a bit of wine in. Or, for the ladies, some wine with a bit of beer in. If you're making this on a date, best put it in a mug or something where you can't see in the sides because it goes sort of grey which is a bit off-puting. Does not work with Guinness, although that's not actually a beer is it?

Mickey Finn

This one's less of a cocktail and more of a thing you can buy off the internet to put in any sort of drink and it'll make you woozy, so it's kind of a universal cocktail. Apparently, a few drops of this makes people forget what they're doing, although that's pretty much what all of my cocktails do so I don't know what all the fuss is about. I might be missing something here.

Turbo Shandy

Bottle of beer, bottle of Smirnoff Ice and a glug of vodka all poured into a pint glass. If anyone ever tells you shandy is a girl's drink, get them to drink two of these and then see what happens. (They'll feel really weird and then puke, that's what'll happen.)

And that's it really. I've just counted them up and realised there are only nine, so when I said I'd easily made ten, I meant nine. So I guess it's back to the lab! Not the actual chemistry lab though, obviously alcohol isn't allowed on school premises. And I have been told to finish by saying that alcohol should be drunk in sensible quantities (of course your definition of "sensible" might be well different to other peoples).

DRINKING GAMES

rules off the warwick uni visit

by ~~Nick~~ NEIL

these games was such good fun i'm writing them down so you can play too and also so i never forget the exact rules. first thing to remember is that you need booze for all of them but if you don't have booze you could use whisky

right these are the the best games that i can remember.

1. FUCKY DUCKS

everyone gets in a circle and then you go round just saying whatever number you can think of. then after a while one of the people playing who is called the bomba deer tells you that you have to drink some of your booze. then you keep going round or something and then the last one to say fucky ducks is the loser and has to drink all their booze. and then the winner has to drink all their booze. and then everyone else has to drink all their booze as well.

2. ORANGEADE AND FAG BUTS GAME

basically you drink most of a big bottle of orangeade but leave a bit in the bottom then get everyone to stick their old fag butts in it for about an hour. at the end of the time limit the guy called admiral says you have to drink it and then you drink it. i won that game easy. the trick is to just drink it really.

3. Tooth Fingers

so what you do in this game is everyone has a drink of booze, right, and then if you do something wrong that is against the rules of the game they all shout "tooth fingers" and then you have to have some of your drink roughly about three centimetres of it. then you keep going till someone chunders on their trousers and then everyone gets bored and starts a new drinking game.

4. DOWN it

so there's this guy called the duckmaster general and sometimes for no reason he just shouts "down it! down it!" and then you have to drink your whole drink. and so does everyone else. the winner is the one who is the duckmaster general from the start of the game.

whoever is the most annoying nob in the room has to eat a toy tree while you laugh at them and that's the sign to start drinking.

5. EATING THE BONZAI TREE

Rudge Park Comprehensive School

End of Year Staff Appraisal

Member of Staff name: Phillip Gilbert

Position held: Head of sixth form

Institution: Rudge Park Comprehensive School

Assessor: Mr. L. Hopkins MEd (head)

Staff photo:

Important note:

The acting headmaster should, in the boxes below, briefly summarise the staff member's performance with regards to each specific heading, starting here with his/her record of achievement over the preceding school year.

Overall notes:

We like to encourage a variety of teaching styles at Rudge Park and I am always keen to observe Phillip's unique and, as some would say, laissez-faire approach to running a sixth form.
He is very confident and knows where to draw the line with students – even though the rest of us would draw that line somewhere completely different.

Areas for improvement:

Headmaster's observations:
It takes time to garner respect from certain elements within the school community. Phillip has, on occasion, seen fit to employ a robust and forthright manner with the pupils in an attempt to accelerate this process – an approach I don't wholeheartedly support. What I'm saying is Phillip, the pupils are sensitive souls and if they feel too victimised they can over-react and make silly, but irreversible, decisions.

Employee's response:

This is a great observation, one that I assume was made from the safety of the ivory tower in which senior staff live. If it pleases the school I will happily sit back and watch students enter this place as morons... and leave as total imbeciles. However, because I consider teaching to involve some level of engagement – and since there is no A-Level in "common sense" (yet) – I have decided to actively pass on my many, many years of acquired knowledge to the students whether they ask for it or not. And yes, some students may get more of my attention than others in this regard, but rest assured that I only impart it to the pupils with the thickest of skulls.

Management of student behaviour:

Headmaster's observations:

The sixth form as a whole has been showing a great improvement this year. I would like to think this is a direct result of Phillip's hard work and constant... let's call it "encouragement". (Although "encouraging" the children to stay in exams when their bowels are struck with an embarrassing illness may be a step too far.)

I believe Phillip has also been getting to know the students' parents very well – and I think this interest in keeping families involved is to be commended. But I request that when talking to the students Phillip avoid making inappropriate comments about their mothers.

On the pastoral side, sixth formers continue to look up to Phillip. Away from the classroom, the inaugural Christmas Prom was, in Phillip's own words, "not a complete disaster".

Employee's response:

Yes I am brilliant, aren't I? I'm probably eligible for a teaching medal or perhaps an engraved pen. I do think the students should always be "encouraged". I believe that the students should knuckle down and ideally not talk to me. Plus, this is a school last time I checked, and at this school my name is "Mr Gilbert" not "Phil". If the diarrhoea-stricken child in question had called me by the right name, he may not have ended up in the "mess" he found himself in.

With regards to McKenzie's mother I was merely stating a fact. I did not state any intention. She is very much my type, but it's funny how my students only remember facts like that rather than the thousands of other facts we try to teach them daily.

And finally, yes, the prom wasn't a complete disaster. In defence of the boy who soiled himself to the laughter of all the other students during his exam, he did organise a fairly innocuous 'jamboree' of adolescent nonsense. Well done him.

And well done me.

Long term goals:

Headmaster's observations:

Phillip should continue his excellent work with the pupils of Rudge Park. He should also pay close attention to his ongoing mentoring of the geography department's John Kennedy who, I am reliably informed, is responding well to his treatment.

Further goals I would like to see Phillip attain are:

- Assigning the correct work experience job to the correct students
- Taking seriously any complaints raised by parents

Employee's response:

I'm afraid the work experience mix-up was a fortunate computer error for which I take no responsibility. But I strongly believe that both students got what they deserved.

And yes, perhaps I shouldn't have laughed at Wills unfortunate swimming trip, and yes I do think his mum is very much my type — but what's done is done. The complaint was acknowledged and I can very much promise that I have spent much time thinking about that incident and "discussing" it with other members of staff/friends/ family/ people I meet at bus stops who look like they're having a bad day.

Signature of Assessor: _L. Hopkins_ (MEd)

Signature of Staff member: _P. Gilbert_

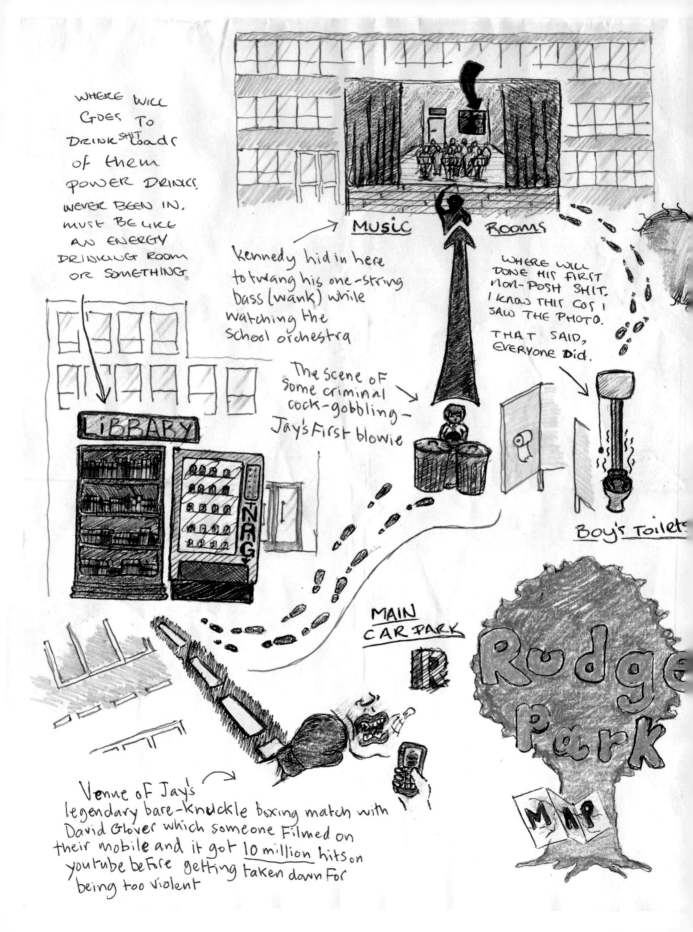

Music

REVIEWS

Music Editor WILLIAM MCKENZIE

Some of Rudge Park's biggest music enthusiasts have kindly agreed (with a little cajoling from you-know-who) to pass their critical eyes and even more critical ears over some of the latest aural delights for the yearbook. Who knows? Perhaps one of these "muso journos" could go on to become the next Steve Lamacq or Lauren Laverne? Or perhaps not...

LIVE REVIEWS

FAILSAFE @ THE ENTERPRISE

I was very much looking forward to the epic choruses, gigantic riffs and anthemic soundscapes which are trademarks of Failsafe, so that makes it all the more unfortunate that I barely got to hear any of their set. One of the reasons for this was the moronic little boys in the mosh pit who seemed intent of hurting people rather than actually listening to the music. Their pathetic pushing games resulted in me missing the last four songs, including "Fire At Will", which is the only one I actually know of theirs, because I had

to nurse my injured nose. To add illness to injury, I was then physically sick, presumably due to the totally gross conditions of The Enterprise's drinks dispensers. What I did hear of Failsafe's set was totally awesome and they rocked, rocked, rocked hard.

By Tara Brown

TAKE THAT'S CONCERT AT WEMBLEY STADIUM

While I normally listen to cool music like Kasabian and Kanye West, I decided to give Take That a try because the person I was going with paid for my ticket. It actually wasn't that bad. If you listen to the songs, they've written some good ones, haven't they? The other thing that was good was there was some really cool props, like a giant metal elephant that actually moved. Even on the songs that nobody knew (mostly the ones off the new album), it wasn't too boring because they had some acrobats and stuff you could watch. When I saw Kasabian at the V Festival on telly, there were quite a few songs I didn't know and it would have been much better if they'd had some jugglers or trapeze artists to distract you on those ones. In summary, it was a really amazing concert, and I think I'd have enjoyed it

even more if our seats hadn't been really far back and to the side so I couldn't even see the big video screens.

In terms of scores, I'd give the gig:

Music: **8/10**   Props: **9/10**   Visibility: **3/10**   Acrobats: **9/10**

Merchandising availability: **10/10**   Catering: **7/10**   Overall: **8/10**   Journey home: **4/10**

By Simon Cooper

WESTLIFE AT WAYNE AND COLEEN ROONEY'S WEDDING, ITALY

This was proper rubbish. Loads of lovey-dovey girly ballads about flying and stuff. Only reason I went was because Wazza invited me over to Italy for the bash and it felt rude not to. After all, he'd come to my 16th so it was only fair. The food was alright and it was nice hanging out with a couple of the England lads I used to play with at West Ham under 13s (even though I was much younger than them, I used to nutmeg them all the time). But the music from those Irish crooning twats was utterly shocking. Wazza should have got me to book the music - I'd have had a word with Liam G and sorted something proper out. After

they'd finished and got booed off, I stepped up and saved the day with a twelve hour non-stop DJ set of epic proportions. Rio said I saved the entire wedding by merking everyone. We just merked left, right and centre all over them. Me and Rio merking. Merking is cool.

By Jay Cartwright

CD REVIEWS

RECURRING DREAM: THE BEST OF CROWDED HOUSE

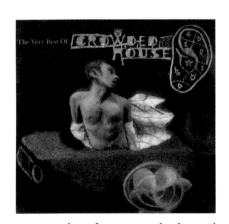

"Weather With You". "World Where You Live". "Fall At Your Feet". Any normal band could retire without any loss of face after writing such masterpieces of contemporary music, and yet these are merely the first four tracks on the album *Recurring Dream*. That is how prolific Crowded House are. It is no wonder their influence is audible in every single decent musical act that has formed since their heyday. There are nineteen tracks in all on this flawless collection and because I waited a few years after it had been released before buying it, I got it online for £1.98 which works out at just over 10p per song. What incredible value. And every song is a hit. If the compilers of the *Now That's What I Call Music* series actually knew anything about credible music, they would be required to fill entire double CDs with only Crowded House songs. If I had to give a negative it would be that this album is that, because it was released in 1996, it doesn't include any of the wonderful new material from their post-reformation albums *Time On Earth* or *Intriguer* (tell me "English Trees" isn't a classic? You can't). Given that *Recurring Dream* is cited as a greatest hits collection, there has clearly been some kind of oversight in the chronology of these albums. But please don't let this annoying technicality spoil your enjoyment of the House.

By Will McKenzie

Patient Report Form

County of

1. Incident Details

Date	16/02	Time	22·16	Hrs

Duty/Location of Incident: THE ENTERPRISE PUB, MONUMENT GREEN, KT13

How Alerted: Self Referral [ ]   Called to Scene [✓]

2. Patient Details

Surname: McKENZIE
Forename/s: WILLIAM
Address: UNKNOWN

Date of Birth: ____   Age: ____   Gender: (M) F

3. General Practitioner

G.P. Name:

Surgery Address:

4. The Problem

ON ARRIVING AT THE SCENE IT BECAME CLEAR THE PATIENT WAS IN A STATE OF MENTAL DISTRESS. HE WAS SWEATING PROFUSELY WHILST COMPLAINING HIS HANDS WERE SAUSAGES AND THAT EVERYTHING WAS FLAT. REPEATE REQUESTS TO SEE HIS MOTHER. NO SIGNS OF EXTERNAL TRAUMA.

5. Primary Survey

Signs of external bleeding   Yes [ ] No [ ]
History of unconsciousness   Yes [ ] No [ ]

6. Medical History

Respiratory [ ]   Cardiac [ ]   Stroke [ ]   Epilepsy [ ]
Diabetes [ ]   Asthma [ ]   High Blood Pressure [ ]

Known Allergies? SOMETHING THEY PUT IN SUPERMARKET READY MEALS BIOLOGICAL WASHING POWDER, SUGAR FREE MINTS, CHOCOLATE, CHEESE, GRASS, SEEDS, CUCUMBER, DUST MITES, WILLOW TREES ETC.

List Regular Medication VICKS VAPORUB APPLIED NIGHTLY BY HIS MOTHER. REGULAR USE OF AN IONISER. REQUESTED ONE FOR HIS HOSP. ROOM. ALSO COUGH SYRUP WAS FOUND ON PREMISES – NO EVIDENCE OF INGESTION.

7. Observations

Time	Hrs							
Pulse Rate	206 BPM – YES MY COLLEAGUE DOUBLE CHECKED WE DIANT BELIEVE IT EITHER							
Respiratory Rate								
Blood Pressure								
Pupil – Patients		Left	Right	Left	Right	Left	Right	Left	Right
Reactive? Yes/No								
Size								

Pupil Sizes
●1mm ●2mm ●3mm ●4mm ●5mm ●6mm ●7mm ●8mm

1 Bleeding   4 Dislocation   7 Pain
2 Burn   5 Embedded Object   8 Swelling
3 Contusion   6 Fracture   9 Wound

NEW FOUND ABILITY TO SMELL COLOURS

Left

Right

INVOLUNTARY ARM SPASMS NECESSITATING THE USE OF RESTRAINT STRAPS

8. Treatment

		Treatment Notes
Airway Opened	[ ]	
Cervical Spine Control	[ ]	
Airway Inserted	[ ]	
Airway Suctioned	[ ]	
Rescue Breaths	[ ]	
Chest Compressions	[ ]	
Wound Cleaned With?	[ ]	
Wound Dressed With?	[ ]	

Head Injury Advice/Card Given   Yes [ ] No [ ]
Tetanus Advice/Card Given   Yes [ ] No [ ]

9. Medical Gases

Oxygen   Yes [ ] No [ ]   Ltr/Min ____ % ____
Analgesic Gas   Yes [ ] No [ ]

Defibrillation

Time of Arrest			Hrs
CPR in Progress	Yes ☐ No ☐		Hrs
Bystander CPR in Progress	Yes ☐ No ☐		Hrs
Shock			Hrs
Shocks Delivered			
Shock			Hrs
Make and ID Number of Defibrillator Used			

11. Vehicle Times (pl...)

Vehicle Call Sign	
Time Call Received	
Time Vehicle Dispatched	
Time Arrived Scene	
Time Left Scene	
Time Arrived Hospital	
Time Available	
Receiving Hospital	
Urgent Call — Scheduled Time of Arrival	
Time Hospital Alerted	

Additional Notes

Notes

THE PATIENT REVEALED HE HAD ORALLY INGESTED A QUANTITY OF HASHISH. NOT AS A DRUG-BASED INGREDIENT OF BAKED GOODS (EG. BROWNIES) BUT WHOLE AND BY ITSELF. HE THEN REASSERTED THE BELIEF HE WAS INSIDE A THICK BUBBLE AND THAT TIME WAS MOVING VERY SLOWLY (IT WASN'T - I CHECKED USING MY DIGITAL WATCH). OTHERWISE HEALTHY - IF HYPERTENSIVE, PARANOID AND PANICKY. ALTHOUGH, ACCORDING TO ONLOOKERS, THIS IS NOT UNCHARACTERISTIC. PATIENT WAS GIVEN FLUIDS, DELIVERED BY AMBULANCE TO HOSPITAL AND ADVISED THAT THE PSYCHOTROPIC EFFECTS OF THE DRUG WILL WEAR OFF IN 48-72 HOURS. NO FURTHER ACTION TAKEN, OTHER THAN TO ADVISE HIM THAT IF HE CONTINUES HIS WRECKLESS USE OF DRUGS, HE WILL DIE YOUNG. BUT IF HE REALLY MUST TAKE NARCOTICS, PROB BEST TO SMOKE THEM LIKE NORMAL TEENAGERS.

Disposal

...vent ☐ Home ☐ Advised to seek medical aid	
☐ Review later ☐ Advised to call NHS Direct	

Transport

...lic ☐ NHS Ambulance ☐ SJA Transport	
...ate) Time Left Unit [ ] Hrs	

14. Handling and Immobilisation

☐ Arm Sling	☐ Box Splint	☐ Vacuum Splint
☐ Cervical Collar	☐ Long Board	☐ Orthopaedic
☐ Carry Sheet	☐ Carry Chair	☐ Stretcher
☐ Blanket	☐ Walked Aided	☐ Walked Unaided
☐ Other (state)		

Drugs/Items Used

	Dose	Batch No.	Time	Signature

17. Treated/Seen By

Print Name	Signature	Role

Declined/Refused Treatment

...offer of treatment and/or transport to ...inst the advice of a member of St. John ...and understand the risk that I am taking.

...nature _____

I confirm that I have explained the treatment/outcome to the patient in terms which he/she, in my judgement, understands.

Member's Signature
(Print name)   JEFFERY BONER

Side A - Driving with the Guys

Driving Nowhere - Hadouken
The passenger - Iggy Pop
Sex on fire - Kings of Leon (Jay's choice)
Chasing Cars - Snow Patrol
Don't dream it's over - Crowded House (Will's choice)
Gone up in flames - Morning Runner
The Hampster dance - Hamilton the Hamster (Neil's choice)
We can Rule the World - Take That (my choice)

Side B - Driving with the Girls

Part 1 - Romance Phase ♥
The Script - The man who can't be moved
Shayne Ward - That's my Goal
Fix you - Coldplay
Will young - All time Love

Part 2 - Action Phase
Hot in here - Nelly
50 cent - Candy shop
Girl I want to make you sweat - UB40
Bump and Grind - R Kelly
Touch me - Rui Da Silva

SIMON'S CAR TAPE ☺

SUNDAY MAY 10th

Last night was supposed to be the big clubbing trip to London. Supposed to be. What a total and utter fucking disaster. It was Will's shitty idea in the first place. I think he finally realised everyone thinks he's a twat and was trying to do a rebrand on himself like when the Rudge Park Jumpers went orange for a term. That failed miserably too. So it's basically all Will's fault for having the idea. Although Jay's to blame for me nearly getting killed by like eight massive blokes who pretty much dragged me out of the car by my neck and mugged me after Jay called them wankers. (Which reminds me, because of our need to get away quickly, we never got the chance to find out if Jay was right about the Tower of London being full of sluts). And Neil's to blame for that horrible smell in my car because he did a piss in my car. Admittedly he tried to get it into a can, but splashback was always inevitable.
But I've forgiven Will, and my neck is getting

better, and I don't even mind about the smell in the Fiat. Dad's gone through 3 bottles of Febreze and had all 4 doors open for 10 hours and still can't get rid of the pissy stench. But that's brilliant cos it means the wanker's down there and not up here bollocking me again (because obviously the more I get bollocked, the more I'll listen – as if...). Mum's just gone quiet. The only reason I wanted to go in the first place was because Carli pretty much said it was a date and that she'd heard I was a great dancer. But when I got there it turned out she was with another guy. I doubt it was a full-on relationship. She's just using him. Maybe even to get at me. Plus she must have been impressed that I was out in a London club.

Alright, so I was wearing tramp's shoes that STANK of piss. And I was late in to the club. And I couldn't give her a lift back home because my car was being

attacked by an angry japanese guy. Who'd
wheelclamped me. Or chinese. or something.
But I don't reckon that's THAT bad. She
might still want to hangout during lunch
break on Monday. Might she? She probably
will, she's cool. We're cool.
Oh God. I still haven't written how I got home.
So Will made me park in this dodgy back
street near the club and I got clamped and
had to call Dad at one in the morning.
That wasn't brilliant but then when he
finally arrived and paid off the angry
Korean guy who might have been from Thailand
actually, I realised I'd had my lights on the
whole time and the battery was flat. So Dad
had to call the AA who took ages to get my
car started again, during which time the
Taiwanish guy had clamped THEIR van. That
was another two hundred quid and
then we had to go home via a hospital
because Neil thought his nob was infected.
His Dad was there like a shot though.

I guess a nob's a nob. So I now owe my Dad £400, and 3 bottles of febreze, plus I need to borrow some money from him to buy some new tramers. But he's said I can pay him back when I get a job, which is brilliant because that'll be ages and by then he'll probably have forgotten. The senile old dick. So everything might be alright.

Call Alan Cooper for more details on
07700 900977

For sale: M-reg Fiat Cinquecento - Special 'Hawaii' edition

Features:

- Four wheels – plus bonus spare tyre in boot!
- "Trendy" yellow paintwork with unique passenger-side feature – door in contrasting rocket-red.
- Retro style Cassette Deck – original feature!
- Engine!
- Wipe-clean seats! (small vanilla yoghurt stain on the back seat)
- Novelty bumper sticker!

Safety Features: The following factors mean that this car is perfect for drivers who would prefer not to be killed in a road accident:

- Speed limiter – the car has been modified so that if it goes above 50mph. It ululates as a warning that you need to slow down.
- Fire Retardant Upholstery – the seats have been slightly moistened using a special kind of lake water which helps to prevent mechanical fires spreading.

Price: £250
or relatively near offer.

SHIT!

To Mr. Gilbert
Rudge Park Comprehensive

24 May.

Dear Mr. Gilbert

I'm writing to you pre-emptively to excuse any erratic behaviour that my son Simon might be about to exhibit.

You see, my company has been making a lot of redundancies recently — you know how it is at the moment. Well, you probably don't because you're a teacher so you're not affected by this kind of real world stuff. But it's tough. And while I've managed to keep my job, I will have to relocate the family abroad, to Swansea. We broke the news to Simon at a family meeting earlier this week and, to be honest, it went down like an excrement sandwich.

As you know, Simon is a sensitive boy and prone to abrupt mood swings. He gets that from his Mum. You know, when Pamela was younger, one minute she'd be having a blazing argument with me, the next we'd be all over each other like randy teenagers on Red Bull. These days though my libido has plateaued a bit whereas Pamela's has, if anything, ramped up. Which is remarkable — God knows I've tried to keep up.

①

So it wouldn't surprise me if you did see Simon acting a bit differently around school. This unsettling experience may well manifest itself in a number of ways. For example, you may hear him being a bit more profane. We've certainly had an increase in the number of f-words, c-words, t-words, v-words and sh-words under our roof, some of them used in very creative ways, which is something at least. And I do remember that Simon's schoolwork suffered the last time we had some problems at home. It was a dark patch and I actually had to move into a hotel for a week because Pamela and I were out of sexual synchronicity with one another. If I'm honest, she just got too much for me for a bit there. We're both very sexual people you see, but Pamela can be vigorous. And when I'm not able to keep up it does cause problems.

So anyway, if you see Simon struggling a bit I'd very much appreciate it if you could cut him some slack, or maybe even bung a few extra percent onto his coursework marks. If he was having a better time at school, I really think it might relieve a bit of pressure at home and could well loosen me up in the bedroom department. I'm having an ~~us~~ unusually dry spell to be honest and lightening the load would be appreciated. At least Pam's not having a dry spell — thank God. Not

③

at all. That's not a problem —yet.

I feel ever so guilty about all of this, and I know it's tough for Simon and Andrew, but honest to God, I just want them to be happy. I love those boys so, so much. Breaks my heart that I have to move them away.

Yours Sincerely,

David A. Cooper.

③

Personal statement worksheet

| Student Name | Simon Cooper |

This section if for your personal statement. Give evidence of the skills you have that are required to study your chosen subject or attain your elected occupation and how you intend to use the knowledge and experience you will gain. Take care to include details of hobbies, interests and any positions of responsibility held and make specific reference to any relevant jobs, placements or work experience undertaken. 4,000 characters max.

Your course

Why are you applying for your chosen course(s)?

Okay, so starting off with a bit of an introduction. My name is Simon Cooper and the reason I want to go to university is that, well, it's just something to do after school, really. It'd be really good to get away from living at home with my parents, because independence is important, isn't it?

I don't really mind which university I go to. It'd be good if I went to somewhere that someone I knew was going to as well. For example, there's a schoolfriend I have called Carli D'Amato and we've been friends since I was 8, so it might be good if I just go to wherever she's going for uni. You know, so we both know someone at the new uni and can share lifts and stuff. Seems like a very good idea, in practical terms. Also she has great taste, and is great.

Why does this course interest you? Include eveidence that you understand what's required to study the course.

Right. So you probably want me to choose a subject now. I'm actually quite open to suggestions on what to study. It's not that I don't care, it's just that I'm not fussy. That's probably helpful, isn't it? You can fit me in wherever there's space. The only preference I have is that I'd rather not do a course that was too male-biased. Which is a shame because engineering actually looks like a career I might enjoy, but that's basically just the next three years sat in a room full of hairy blokes isn't it? So maybe pick me a course where there is a bit more sexual equality in the make up of the class (or even a slight female bias) and also, ideally, one that only has three lectures a week. Art? Sociology? Religious Studies? Actually, thinking about it, I don't want to meet girls who are too religious.

Why do you think you're suitable for the course(s)?

Okay, so "Have I had any positions of responsibility?" Well, no, but then I'm only 18 so that's not really a question for me, is it? I'm still technically a school child, and school children are obviously too young for responsibility. I don't even know why I'm answering this bit really, as it's obviously just for mature students.

Skills and achievements

Universities like to know the skills you have that will help you on the course, or generally with life at university, like any accredited or non-accredited achievements.

Finally, you want to know about work experience. I did do a week on my friend's Dad's plant hire site, but that wasn't really work. It was mainly putting stuff in a skip, with occasional breaks when I'd sit in my car and eat sandwiches. But anyway, the reason you go to uni is so you can eventually get a job, so it doesn't really matter if I haven't done any work yet, does it? Or does it? If it does, I did do work experience, it just wasn't one I'd like to repeat.

Rudge Park Comprehensive School
Work Experience Feedback Form

Student name: Simon Cooper

Company: Cartwright Plant Hire

What were the student's strengths?

Well, he didn't whinge like some of the work experience kids I've had recently, not naming any names (but I'll give you a clue, I'm talking about my son.). Simon didn't mind setting ~~stonk~~ stock in when it came to chucking stuff into a skip and I was very proud of the lad. It was like working with the son I never had.

What were the student's weaknesses?

Lack of a coat. Simon spent most of the week shivering like a humping dog. It wasn't even that cold, but he and Jay insisted on dressing like a low rent JLS.

What are the student's areas for improvement?

Simon should start by getting a heavy-duty coat. or any sort of coat really. Try Millets. once he's got a coat, he should get himself some new friends and stop hanging round with my boy — I'm not being mean but Jay's dragging him down. sometimes I honestly wonder where I went wrong with that lad.

Name and position for the organisation:

Terry Cartwright   Owner.

What did you enjoy about your placement?

I didn't really enjoy very much to be honest. My friend Jay who organised the placement sort of said it would be fun and it really wasn't. It was cold. Being away from my parents for eight hours was good though. Plus it gave me time to contemplate the things I really want to do in the future an how I plan to do them.

What didn't you enjoy about your placement?

Well I certainly didn't enjoy driving diggers or jumping them over cement mixers and that's because I didn't get to drive any diggers or jump them over cement mixers. Not that I would have expected to be able to drive diggers and jump them over cement mixers had Jay not said that's what we'd spend most of our time doing. He also said we'd get paid a grand each at the end of the week and that didn't happen either. Basically, everything I'd hoped it was going to be and was told it was going to be. It wasn't.

What did you learn from your work experience?

Not to believe anything Jay says. Ever. Also I suppose I learnt that working outside is quite cold. So outside's not a good place to work. And there are no computers outside so it's quite hard to check Facebook or go on Wikipedia to prove that everything Jay's talking about is bollocks.

Has your work experience aided your career choices?

The placement has made a valuable contribution to my careers outlook because I'm definitely not going to do any kind of outdoors job. It made me realise what I want to do with my life, and that's get a job indoors. Probably not with Jay either.

Signature of student:

Simon Cooper

Rudge Park Comprehensive School
Student end of year report: Deputy Head's assessment

Student name: SIMON COOPER   **Year:** 6th Form

"Simon Cooper has been an absolute joy to tutor this year." Perhaps that's a bit strong. Yes, it is very strong actually. But he certainly hasn't been a nuisance and that alone gives him a distinct advantage over nearly every other member of Rudge Park upper sixth form. If only more adolescent children were like Simon, my job would be immeasurably easier. And possibly even vaguely enjoyable. Sadly, however, one swallow does not a summer make — although six and a half weeks of paid holiday with no marking most certainly does.

Simon would no doubt benefit from a little more self-confidence and a lot less hair gel, but I understand that's the fashion these days and, despite my misgivings, he doesn't seem to get bullied for his appearance. When I was at school, they would have gone to town on his pointy hair-do, probably reducing him to tears and maybe even self harm. But things change, sometimes for the better.

Like Simon's behaviour. Very early on, he set a precedent for being an ingenious mischief-maker. Phoning me personally mid-morning and impersonating his own mother, in a desperate bid to play truant for a day early in his first term was, I came to learn, very uncharacteristic. I would have happily given Simon the benefit of the doubt and assumed he'd been put up to the prank by one of his less scrupulous friends, but unfortunately the head caught wind of it and things got blown out of all proportion. Simon is essentially a good boy at heart, something I've taken great pains to avoid telling him on several occasions.

Signature:

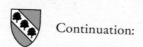

Continuation:

Now, I understand from the letters I've received that there's been some sort of unrest at home, but let me assure you that Simon's classwork has been consistently adequate, and his behaviour no more or less erratic than I've come to expect from the hormonally-ravaged rabble under my care. There was one incident during the school charity fashion show where — be it due to a fragile mind, some sort of dare, or simply a misguided attempt to raise awareness of testicular cancer, — Simon exposed himself to more than a hundred parents, teachers and fellow pupils. But I am very glad to report this hasn't been the start of a trend and Simon has kept himself firmly to himself since. Especially with regards to members of the opposite sex, whom he appears to view (from a distance) with a mixture of terror and utter resignation.

But let me be clear, I'd rather that this sort of lovestruck mooning was the norm than some of the regrettable incidents brought to my attention on almost a weekly basis by the school cleaners. They get paid even less than I do and should not have to see what they've seen. Believe me, I've had two-hour meetings about purchasing sturdier gloves for the weekend cleaners and, to this day, one of the older ladies still refuses to enter the second-floor boys' toilet.

But I digress. Simon is a well-meaning boy who just lacks ambition. And direction. Two things which, when combined, can only lead to one place: the University of Lincoln. And trust me, he does not want to end up there.

Signature: P. Gilbert

From: SimonCooper@TheCooperFamily.org.uk
To: PatriceMakeTheSex@hotmail.fr
Subject: Bon Jour Patrise

Salut Patrise,

Je vous writing pour vous to see how you're doing now you're back in France. All okay avec vous? Actually, I'm going to write in English now, because you need to learn this.

So anyway, back here, things are going pretty merde for me. Carli is still going out with that massif dickhead Tom. She obviously can't see what the rest of us see - that having a car and being 6 foot 3 and playing rugby don't necessarily stop you from being a prick.

Mon dieu, I wish I could just tell her what I feel about her. If I was French like you and didn't care about what people thought about how I looked like or behaved, and was much more obsessed with sex and less bothered about getting a reputation for being sleazy, this would be so much easier.

Maybe I should buy a leather jacket and start smoking. I could just smoke menthols - it'd still look cool. Could you maybe send me some cigarettes? Cool ones. She clearly isn't into me as "normal" Simon - so maybe she'd go for menthol Simon?

Anyway, I'm nearly at the end of my hour's internet daily allowance (bloody parents), so I will say au revoir for now.

Simon.

From: PatriceMakeTheSex@hotmail.fr
To: SimonCooper@TheCooperFamily.org.uk
Subject: Re: Bon Jour Patrise

Hi Simon,

It is funny that this email you send me now because I was just doing a
masturbation when the message was arriving at my computer and my sex
thoughts to keep my head erotic were about your friend Will's mother.
What a coincidence is that! She is on Facebook.

Actually, I having am some tiny problem with my sex thoughts as I can not
exactly remember cup size of Will's mother's breasts and I would hate it if my
sex thoughts were being not so accurate, yes? So please find out the tit size
for me, yes? Thank you. And also for similar reasoning you could please find
out the height in metres of your school friend Charlotte Hinchcliffe and also
her natural colour of hair as well? We left the lightbulb turned up, but many of
her sex parts were under duvet so I did not see for certain the colour. For the
vagina, you understand.

I have sexed many girls, naturally, so perhaps I can help you with some advice
to help you sex Carli. Do not smoke the menthol cigarettes, because they are
smoked only by the pussies. Smoke the real cigarettes and just when you are
at party with her and she is having a good time whisper in her ear that you
think she has sex and you would like to take her upstairs and do lover her.
That exact thing worked for me with Charlotte who is also English girl, so it
will work with Carli for sure.

I will answer you question concerning how things are with me, well, not so
good. My father did dying yesterday because of the cancer for the lungs and
he was only 44 old.

Goodbye,

Patrice

PS. You spell my name wrong.

From: SimonCooper@TheCooperFamily.org.uk
To: PatriceMakeTheSex@hotmail.fr
Subject: Re: Re: Bon Jour Patrise

Allo Allo Patrise,

Great to hear votre news and glad that life is going well for you!

So I tried to take your advice about Carli, but unfortunately there has only been one party that she's gone to and Tom was there with her. And I wasn't invited to it anyway. What do you French guys do when you the girl you love has a lanky dickhead for a boyfriend and you never get invited to the parties they go to?

I'm beginning to wonder if I'm just destined to be alone my whole life - that I'll spend decades watching Carli from a distance as she dates moron after moron, because she's too blind to see that the love of her life has been her best friend since she was 8. That would be a real tragedy.

I'll sign off now as I'm nearly at the end of my internet allowance again - bloody fucking stupid parents. I wish they'd just fuck off and die sometimes.

Au revoir,

Simon.

PS - Couple of quick questions; where did you buy your leather jacket from? What brand of cigarettes do you smoke? How long did it take to grow your hair that long?

From: PatriceMakeTheSex@hotmail.fr
To: SimonCooper@TheCooperFamily.org.uk
Subject: Re: Re: Re: Bon Jour Patrise

Simon,

I am sad to hear all about your internet allowance and your badly sex attempts to Carli. My sympathy is with you very much.

Life here is tough because my father did dying, and the sadness in my soul is a manifestation by me doing the bad things very more than ever ever I have before. Have you read Camus? L'Etranger, c'est moi. I am now smoked a day 60 cigarettes, I am drink a bottle wine every morning and I am tug 5 to 9 times all days - but still the sadness is remaining. At night I sleep not at all and as I stare into nothing, I cry the tears, then more tug, then cry.

My jacket is buyed from author in French bar. I smoke Camel. My hair is always being this long.

From Facebook pictures of Will's mother I make guess she has in English a DD bosoms, in France a 90E. Email me if you think disagree with my estimation. I also am choosing estimate that Charlotte is brunette hair but only she dyes her top hair.

Goodbye,

Patrice

PS. You still spell my name wrong.

A Message from Alistair

By William McKenzie
Yearbook Editor

One of the most memorable events of this academic year was without doubt the Charity Fashion Show, ably organised by Carli D'Amato. I think we can all agree that it provided many significant talking points.

But while some might consider a fashion show to be a narcissistic method of raising money for charity, and others might even go as far as saying that the selfishness of instigating such an event actually outweighs the vain attempt at selflessness, the masses still seemed to think it was a worthwhile event.

The beneficiary of this fundraising extravaganza was Rudge Park pupil Alistair Scott, whose long term illness has provided us all with a pertinent reminder that whatever you might think of someone, no one deserves to get kidney failure.

While there really is no need for Alistair to thank us all for our hard work leading up to the event and on the night itself, he felt the need to do so anyway and, despite my remonstrations that it was most definitely was unnecessary, Mr Gilbert agreed with Alistair.

Given that Alistair is no doubt taking a cocktail of prescription drugs as part of his courageous recovery, it's likely that some of his musings may be factually inaccurate and possibly even libellous. Let's leave that for the lawyers to decide.

With all of that in mind, here is Alistair's thank you to us, his fellow schoolmates.

Dear fellow Rudge Park pupils,

Super thank yous all for your fantabulous efforts and kindness at the Charity Fashion Show! When I heard that you guys were staging such a brill fundraising event, I just felt utterly amazeballs.

There are a few people I would like to single out for super-special thanks. Firstly, the gorgeous Carli D'Amato for her wonderful organisational skills, her beautiful caring soul and also for just being a sexy babe! Any guy would feel lucky to merely be in the presence of such a beautiful, horny woman, but to have her dedicate hours to an event to help out an ill lad like me – let me tell you, it's just feels utterly wowzeroony! Love you Carls!

Next I'd like to thank special guest Charlotte Hinchcliffe, who travelled all the way back from university just to put on some raunchy clothes for little old me! What a lucky boy I am. Now you might not know this, because she is so incredibly modest, but it will probably come as no surprise that Charlotte actually used to do some catalogue modelling. So for her to exhibit her talents on stage for free to raise money for me. Well, just mega thanks Charls, you lovely sexy babe, you!

And thankzeroony to all the girls who modelled on the night! Let me tell you this: when I was in hospital with my kidney failure Christine Bleakley visited the ward, and even though she is one of the hottest women in the world, each one of you girls is even sexier than her.

Thank you also to those who toiled away tirelessly behind the scenes; especially Mr Kennedy and Neil Sutherland who worked very closely together, plus the male models who, while they may not have been anything like as attractive as their female counterparts, were adequate in all but one case.

Finally, I'd like to round this off with an inspirational message for all you girls: whoever you end up with in your love life, just make sure it's not the kind of nasty, spoilt little idiot who wears blazers and is mean to people with serious illnesses.

Much love (to the girls, natch!)

Alistair

Alistair Scott

AFTER SCHOOL CLUB NOTICES

Expand your mind! Broaden your horizons! Try something new! Come along! It's fun! And free!

TUESDAY AFTER SCHOOL
Massage club

Relax and unwind and learn the ancient art of the East with keen massage enthusiast Mr. Kennedy. No experience necessary. Oils provided.

CANCELLED DUE TO LOW ATTENDANCE

WEDNESDAY AFTER SCHOOL
Art club

New for the Easter term! Express yourself and learn all about form and colour in a relaxed and welcoming atmosphere. This term we'll be focussing on life drawing. Oils provided. Models required – please contact Mr. Kennedy.

CANCELLED DUE TO LACK OF INTEREST

THURSDAY AFTER SCHOOL
Greco-Roman wrestling club

Hold! Slam! Throw! Better than WWE and tougher than boxing – this one's not for the faint-hearted. Come and discover how the Romans used to unwind – and get fit for summer! One-on-one sessions available with Mr. Kennedy. Sports kit (shorts only) required. Oils provided.

ALWAYS PLENTY OF ROOM! STILL NOT SURE? WHY NOT COME AND WATCH ME AND NEIL GRAPPLE?

BEHIND THE SCENES: THE CHARITY FASHION SHOW

Carli D'Amato, co-ordinator of this year's Charity Fashion Show, gives us the lowdown on how the highly original collections were designed for the charitable, but some might say ethically questionable (due to the marginalisation of those pupils who were not deemed aesthetically pleasing) event.

66 It was a real privilege for me to organise the Rudge Park Fashion Show get a chance to prove that wearing great clothes doesn't have to just COST money – it can RAISE money too! And how being dressed to kill can actually SAVE lives (it's OK – Alistair came up with that himself. So funny! He should be a stand-up. Or a sit-down – at least until his kidneys are better).

Since then, loads of people have asked where I got the ideas for my collections from so I thought I'd give you a little peek into the creative side. A behind the scenes extra! So, on the next few pages, are the "mood boards" I put together for two of the collections that I premiered at the show, as well as the draft sketches for the accompanying designs. 99

"Sexy" Collection

The aim of this "sexy" range is to break rules in all directions, but within conventions.
To be provocative, to be challenging, to be risque. To define the essence of masculinity and femininity all at once. To be human.

CASINO ROYALE

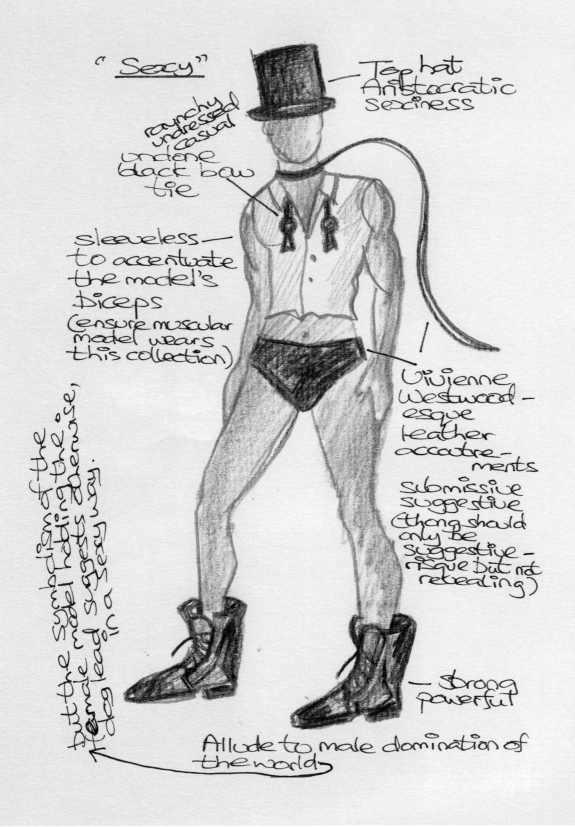

"Sexy"

Top hat
Aristocratic
sexiness

raunchy
undressed
casual
undone
black bow
tie

sleeveless —
to accentuate
the model's
biceps
(ensure muscular
model wears
this collection)

Vivienne
Westwood-
esque
leather
accoutre-
ments
submissive
suggestive
(thong should
only be
suggestive —
risque but not
revealing)

strong
powerful

but the symbolism of the
female model holding the
male model suggests otherwise,
dog lead suggests dominance in a sexy way.

Allude to male domination of
the world

"Glamorous Nights" Collection

Elegance. Dusk. Allure. Moonlight. Fascination. This is the kind of imagery I hope to conjure with my "Glamorous Nights" collection.

"Glamorous"
Feathered hat
to be worn slantily
and sexily

Pink feather boa
to really ramp up the
sexy finale

Corset
to keep
it tasteful

whip/leash
to lead boy
partner

Parisian.
/mysterious
Alluring heel shape.

14th June - WORST fucking day of my life!!

So the charity fashion show was yesterday. What a total and fucking disaster. Everything was going brilliantly. Carli even said, and these are her exact words, that I had an "utterly amazing hot body". But apparently that doesn't extend to my left bollock which ACCIDENTALLY popped out by ACCIDENT and now everyone's acting like, I dunno, like I had a pop at that wheelchair-bound dick Alastair. In fact it was all Will who had a go at him, and it was deliberate, but he didn't get in trouble at all. So fucking unfair. Although now everyone's calling Will "Speccy spaz-hater" which Will doesn't like for one because technically Alastair isn't a spaz. He is still a dick though.

Anyway Gilbert's gone apeshit about my testicle show and he gave me a right bollocking, which is ironic. And even though I'm not in trouble at home, Dad's already started calling me Bobby Ball. Whoever that is. So fucking unfunny.

The well unfair thing is that it was all Neil's fault anyway. If he'd done his job properly and helped me get dressed, none of this would have happened. According to Will, lots of people are asking for refunds now. That's a bit off - you can't take money back from charity, can you? And anyway, In strip clubs you probably have to pay more to see what's under the pants. Admittedly, that's usually flange and not sack. So if you think about it, the audience got a good deal really. Regardless, Will's refusing to refund anyone - something to do with statutory rights and the UK charities Act 1992.

Oh Jesus. I just thought. What am I going to say to Carli tomorrow? "Sorry for ruining your show and ensuring everyone now associates your fashion with my testicle"?

I just hope she liked the look of my left ball - what if she prefers shaved ones? Maybe I should start shaving them? What a fucking disaster.

Honestly tonight could not have gone any worse. Actually yes it could - it could have been my right bollock on show. The weird one.

Ψ Millfield Psychiatric Clinic
Patient notes and evaluation

Name	"Jay" Cartwright	Reference	JC/AS01/2305

Age	18	Date	23.05.09

- ## Reason for referral

Parents concerned about their son's mental health. They report that he suffers from delusional tendencies and suspect his obsession with sexual thought and self-pleasure is preventing him from leading an ordinary, fulfilling life.

It is the parents' sincere wish that the clinic might attribute all of Jay's behavioural issues to "learning difficulties" or ADHD or dyslexia "like middle class birds" so that they've "at least got a medical excuse for him".

- ## Mental Status Evaluation

The patient is only just emerging from puberty, a time of life when normal and abnormal behaviours are especially difficult to evaluate.

As part of this initial evaluation, I asked the patient to analyse 20 Rorschach inkblot images. He likened 17 of these images to the vagina and the remaining 3 to elements around or inside the vagina. This indicates a strong preoccupation with sexual activity. Worth noting however that Jay did not use the word "vagina" to describe his visualisations. Instead he used an array of childlike slang for the female pudendum, including (and I quote) "fanny", "snatch", "gash" and "clunge". This is not to say he wasn't polite, he was incredibly polite.

This kind of language typically indicates that the patient is severely sexually immature. His problems appear to stem from the following contradiction: he has the body of a man, the sexual knowledge of a teenager, but the social intelligence of an eight-year-old boy.

- Patient Interview

In an attempt to evaluate the root causes of the patient's behaviours, I attempted to engage him in discussion about his own sexual past. Jay's parents estimate that he self-pleasures up to nine times daily. On presenting this estimate to the patient, he flatly denied it – and then countered by claiming he does indeed ejaculate up to nine times a day, but not alone, because he mostly does it into, and onto, willing female partners.

I then asked how many sexual partners Jay had had, and he said he'd lost count. I asked him to describe some of these sexual partners but interestingly his descriptions were quite vague, atypical for the sort of sexual behaviour he claims to partake in. This leads me to believe that the patient is either so emotionally disconnected that he has no empathy towards his sexual conquests, or that he suffers from massive delusions.

I went on to ask Jay if he sometimes feels he's delusional. He told me that he knew I'd suggest that, because that's what his last psychiatrist, the one who sorted out Stephen Fry and cost £20,000 a session, told him too.

To determine the cause of Jay's issues I focused much of the session on his childhood. He had little to say about his mother, but exhibited an amount of repressed anger towards his father. Unprompted, Jay also began to tell me about a "game" he used to play in his neighbour's shed, but stopped himself before adding much detail. I encouraged him to expand on this further, but the patient simply changed the subject to how he'd like to "do" my receptionist.

- Next steps

Jay's sexual fixation, his socially inappropriate vocabulary, and his delusional psychosis all require outpatient care and attention.

Unfortunately for the patient's parents, it is not my opinion that any of his strange behaviours can be attributed to a readily characterised mental or physical disorder. I would willingly diagnose him with something, but when it comes down to it he is not mentally ill, he's just an exceptionally strange and slightly perverted teenage boy.

Signature of attending therapist:

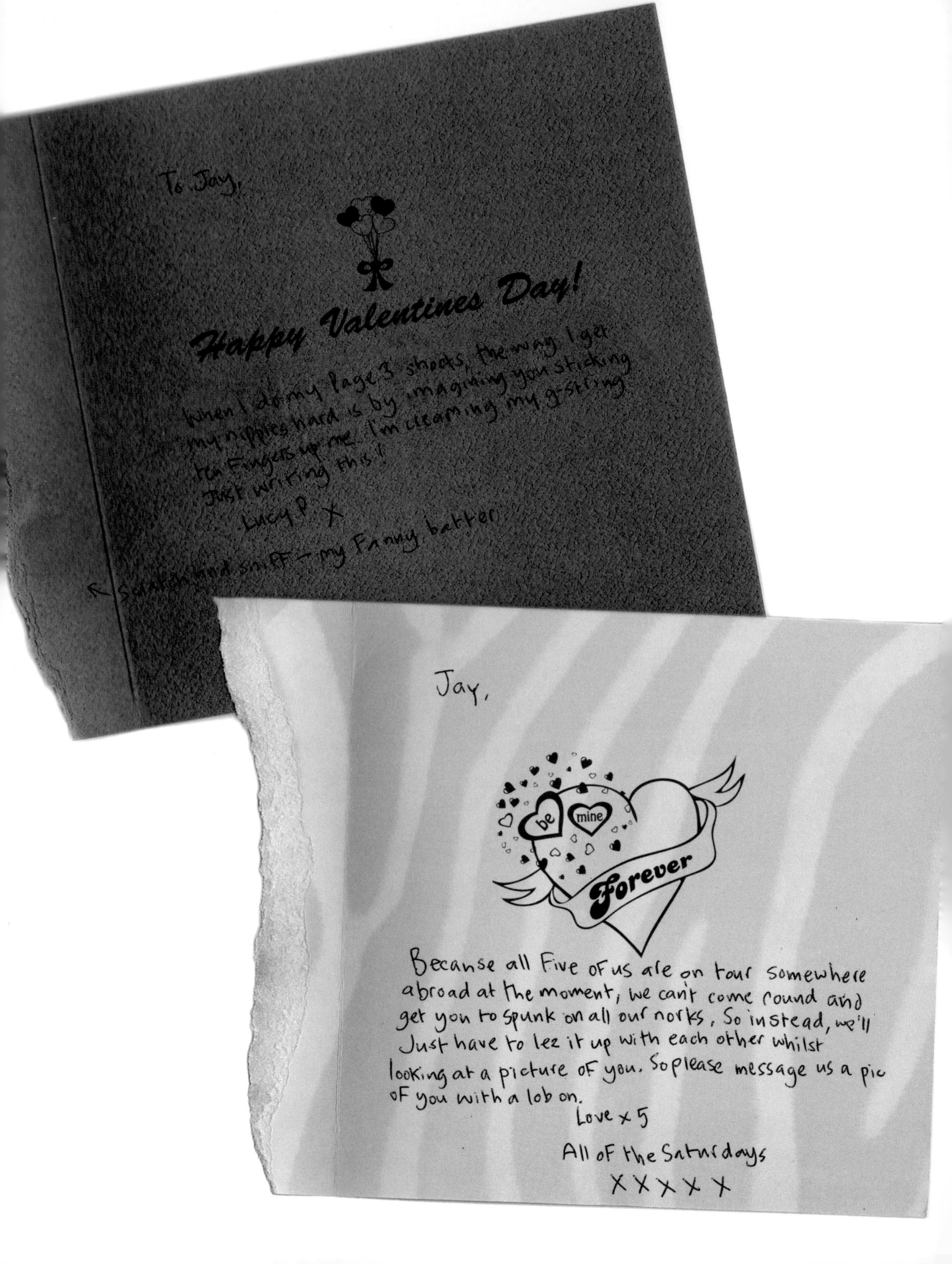

To Jay,

Happy Valentines Day!

When I do my page 3 shoots, the way I get my nipples hard is by imagining you sticking your fingers up me. I'm creaming my g-string just writing this!!

Lucy P. X

P.S santas and sniff — my fanny butter.

Jay,

Because all five of us are on tour somewhere abroad at the moment, we can't come round and get you to spunk on all our norks, so instead, we'll just have to lez it up with each other whilst looking at a picture of you. So please message us a pic of you with a lob on.

Love x 5

All of the Saturdays

X X X X

Our darling Jay,

I want to spend every moment by your side

Happy Valentine's Day, what! Next time you're in London yah, please visit us again at grandmama's palace and we'll go down the bottom of the garden by all the ponies and swans. Then you can give one of us a right royal seeing-to while the other one watches and flicks her bean, Then we'll stop for some tea and scones before swapping over. Just like last time. I'll wear the hat.

Ruddy well can't wait
Beatrice and Eugenie
+ x + x + x + x

Alreet Jay,

On this canny special Valentine's day, I want yous to shoot yer wad inside me. In which ever hole you want, pet.

"you are my hearts desire"

Cheryl C
x + x x x + x

PS. I'm trying to get wor Simon to bring X-Factor anditions to Rudge Park Sports hall so I can nosh yous off in me lunch break.

Little wittle Jay-y-Kins

be my
Valentine...

You rock my world. Please start a band →
I've been asking for ages. You're totally talented
enough. Start a band, right, and then I'll get
you on my Radio 1 show and then, get this, I'll
like put on a really, really, really, REALLY long record
so that you and me can have wicked mega-sex
right there in the Live Lounge in my swimming
costume, that one in that picture you like.
 Do it for me. God I'm horny. You fucking stud.

Fearne C
xxxx

From: ClungeKing@hotmail.com
To: Chloe@TheMaddenFamily.co.uk
Date: 28th June 2009 at 20:30
Subject: Hey babe

Alright babe. Just emailing you to see what you're up to and where you are. Cos I care, you know?

Love ya babes,

Jay-Jay
xxx

From: ClungeKing@hotmail.com
To: Chloe@TheMaddenFamily.co.uk
Date: 28th June 2009 at 20:40
Subject: Re: Hey babe

Alright babe.
Just checking you got my email from before. If you did get it, where were you when you got it and who were you with? I'm interested in your life, like a sensitive boyfriend should be. The reason I want to know what's going on with you is cos I love all those stories about stuff like your mate falling out with your other mate and then them saying something back, then the other one saying something also, then them getting back friends again.

Anyway, let me know where you are and what you're up to as soon as you get this.

Love ya loads babes!

Jay-Jay
xxxoxoxx

PS. Out of interest, you don't remember someone called David Glover do you?

From: Chloe@TheMaddenFamily.co.uk
To: ClungeKing@hotmail.com
Date: 29th June 2009 at 18:30
Subject: Re: Hey babe

Hi Jay,

I just read your Facebook and two Bebo messages about checking I'd got
this email from last night. I hadn't actually because for some reason it got
caught in my junk folder - my computer seems to think your email address
is spam! (Actually what does clungeking mean? Is it from a film?).

In answer to your questions, I've been revising at home - same as the last
few weeks. But thanks for checking I'm okay.

The name David Glover rings a bell - is it someone you've mentioned
before, or is he someone I know?

By the way, thanks for clicking "Like" on every single Facebook photo
of me and leaving comments. Must have taken you ages to do all 436.
There's really no need to keep doing it though, okay?

Chloe x

From: ClungeKing@hotmail.com
To: Chloe@TheMaddenFamily.co.uk
Date: 29th June 2009 at 18:34
Subject: Re: Hey babe

Alright Chloe,

Funnily enough, I was just sitting at my computer and checking my
email was working at the exact moment your email came through, so
that's the reason why I've been able to reply so quickly!

Don't worry about that David Glover thing. He wouldn't be anyone important to you if you don't even remember where you know his name from, would he? And he's not one of your Facebook friends by the looks of things, so just forget I mentioned anything babe.

You have got quite a lot of friends on Facebook, haven't you? 440 in all, Miss Popularity! That's 261 girls and 179 blokes. So not as many blokes as girls, but some would say that's still quite a lot of blokes given that you're in a relationship now - as you say so yourself in your status. By the way, did you know as well as saying you're "in a relationship", you can also add my name to that bit so people know who you're going out with?

Glad you're still revising hard and at home. Best place to revise, really. I think you should stay there really and not head over to Simon Davies's house for that group revision session like he suggested on his wall post to you.
Love you big time, babes!

Jay-Jay
xxxoxoxoooxo

From: ClungeKing@hotmail.com
To: Chloe@TheMaddenFamily.co.uk
Date: 29th June 2009 at 18:39
Subject: Re: Hey babe

Hey Chlo,

Just checking that last email came through okay. Did you get it? Been having problems with the old internet here, and you haven't replied yet.

Big love babes!

Jay-Jay

xxxxooooxxxxoooox

PS. You're not at Simon Davies' house are you?

From: ClungeKing@hotmail.com
To: Chloe@TheMaddenFamily.co.uk
Date: 29th June 2009 at 18:44
Subject: Re: Hey babe

Chloe babe!

Just tried calling you to check if you did get that email or not, but it went to voicemail like seven times in a row. Maybe your voicemail settings are broken. Or have you lost your phone? Or is it out of battery? Or are you with someone who doesn't want you to take the call?

If you want me to come over and help, I could bring my charger or help you find your phone. Or if it's the voicemail thing, I could always help you with that - I could set up a new pin code and keep note of it for you. I could maybe even record a funny answerphone message for you! "Hi, this is Chloe's fella Jay! Leave my missus a message after the tone...". That'd be well funny!

Laterz sexy!

Jay-Jay

XXXOOOXXXXOOOXXX

From: Chloe@TheMaddenFamily.co.uk
To: ClungeKing@hotmail.com
Date: 30th June 2009 at 11:30
Subject: Re: Hey babe

Jay,

I have been trying to revise without the distractions of the computer and my mobile phone. But yes, I got your emails. And your messages and texts. So your email and my voicemail are both working. I also got that note you put through the letterbox. And the flowers you left on the doorstep to wish me a "Happy Revision Session", that was sweet, but you didn't need to.

Will be having an evening off tomorrow night after my exam. Maybe we could meet in person for a drink and talk about a few things?

Chloe

From: ClungeKing@hotmail.com
To: Chloe@TheMaddenFamily.co.uk
Date: 30th June 2009 at 11:33
Subject: Re: Hey babe

Chloesy-babe!

Ah right! I think I know what you mean. Or at least I think I do. I'll make sure I come prepared in case I'm right, because as you know I am the responsible boyfriend type!

Miss you babes. Looking forward to seeing you tomorrow. I've got a night with the lads planned tonight, so expect fewer texts and Bebo messages from me than usual.

Your Man,

Jay-Jay
XOXOXOXOXOXOX

PS. Just to quickly go back to the David Glover thing. He's about 6 foot, brown hair, earring. Are you doubly doubly sure you don't know him? I wouldn't have thought you did, but just double double checking!

The new Social Secretary posts for next year will be taken on by Thessa and Jim Ellis, while the position of chief swordsman will be taken by Jay Cartwright. This will come as no surprise to you because he has been top of the caravan shagging league for the last six years. His responsibilities will entail boning any new Caravan Club birds that he fancies.

I am sure that this will be a popular appointment.

CAMBER SANDS 'CARAVAN CLUB

AUTUMN NEWSLETTER

CARAVAN CLUB NEWS

CARAVAN CLUB NEWS

Dear Member,

Welcome to the autumn newsletter and as usual it has been another splendid summer for the Camber Sands Caravan Club! For the fifth year in a row, there have been increases in the number of orgies in the main hall, mainly because there are now so many fit birds coming here who are desperate to get fingered and banged. In fact at one point last year there wasn't enough nob to go

around so the girls had to start lezzing up - even sisters and twins. But that's all OK here - no-one gets judged. Apart from on their

horniness. On average, every bloke who stayed for a week was involved in 6 threesomes which means that this caravan club is statistically the

easiest place to get a shag in the world.

But please, keep all this sex stuff to yourselves because otherwise every little teenage virgin round the country will descend on this place, and there'll be less humping for the rest of us. Cheers.

Thank you for respecting these wishes, as it will result in many more enjoyable experiences for all of us.

So, till the winter newsletter; Keep caravanning!

Glenn Roberts
Head of Camber Sands Caravan Club

You are cordially invited to join Master W. McKenzie for cocktails and dinner on the eve of Friday 15th May 2009 to celebrate his 17th birthday.

AT WHEN?
7:00pm - Cocktails
7:30pm - Seated for dinner
7:45pm - Starters served
8:00pm - Main course served
8:25pm - Sorbet served
8:35pm - Dessert served
9:00pm - Cheese plate served
9:30pm - Exit from venue quietly

BUT WHERE?
Chez McKenzie (my house)

TO WEAR?
Lounge suits for the gentlemen, evening wear for the ladies. No sportswear or caps.

STRICTLY INVITE ONLY
PBAB (no spirits or anything stupid)

Also, I'd be delighted if you could bring a lady guest to even the gender bias and ensure that conversational subjects do not become controversial or crude. Ideally, please don't bring any vegetarians though, because 1) it's most likely just a phase and they're probably inconsistent (eg. avoid meat but wear leather shoes) and 2) I'm doing chicken in wine (coq au vin) and that's that.

REPLY HOW?
RSVP in writing (printed/handwritten, not email) to Will McKenzie no later than Wednesday 4th March 2009 please.

Cookery

FOOD, GLORIOUS FOOD

Cookery Editor JOHN WEBSTER

Food aficionado and sixth-form student John Webster shares with us his favourite school meals from his two yummy years here at Rudge Park.

Fish, Chips and Peas, *Friday Sept 5th 2008*

A landmark occasion; my first ever fish-based meal at comprehensive school. Little did I know that fish was actually a staple for Friday dinners and that I would have the joy of devouring the school canteen's battered cod on a weekly basis for the next two years!

The peas were cooked nicely, the chips were fried nicely and the fish tasted nice too. A really nice meal. Just when I thought things couldn't get any better, I discovered that one of the dessert options was green jelly with a segment of fruit in it! Niceness in a bowl.

John's Deliciousness (out of 10) 👍👍👍👍👍👍👍👍👍

153

Hamburgers, *Wednesday (evening) December 17th 2008*

On reflection, this is probably the only occasion I've ever eaten hot food outside of lunch hour but still on school property. How strange! That's because I dined on these hamburgers at the school Christmas Prom. What's more, the idea of serving these burgers was partly mine! So while, objectively, these hamburgers may not have been anything special, the pride that I associated with eating them resulted in them tasting as nice as anything I've ever tasted. And I've tasted some very nice things in my wide and varied culinary experiences.

John's Deliciousness (out of 10) 👍👍👍👍👍👍👍👍👍

John's Deliciousness (out of 10)
👍👍👍👍👍👍👍👍👍

Chilli con Carne,
Friday March 11th 2009

The occasion was Red Nose Day and the canteen staff laid on a special Comic Relief menu consisting of Chilli "Comedy" Carne with "Red Nose" Jelly (not green) for pudding. My first foray into Mexican food. I must admit I was a bit disappointed that they removed the normal Friday fish option to make way for this charity alternative. Nevertheless, the Chilli "Comedy" Carne (actually just chilli con carne with an amusing name) was extremely nice, and the "Red Nose" Jelly (which was just comically-rebranded strawberry jelly) was also apparently very nice although I didn't try it because it wasn't green.

Family Feast, *Monday April 16th 2009*

Not strictly a school meal, but nevertheless to do with school because it was on the school trip to Swanage. We stopped off at the service facilities near Fleet on the M3 and were allowed to dine in whichever eatery we favoured. Having never been in a position to eat any variation of southern fried chicken before (due to my parents' culinary preferences for me), I took the opportunity to sample some Kentucky Fried Chicken. For years I had watched their mouth-watering adverts and imagined what their subtle blend of herbs and spices must taste like – and I wasn't disappointed! To maximise this opportunity, I opted for a dish entitled Family Feast meal. The chicken was very nice, the chips were nice, the ketchup was really nice and the Vienetta was deliciously nice.

John's Deliciousness (out of 10) 👍👍👍👍👍👍👍👍👍

Dr Wilson
Longford School for Boys

Dear Dr Wilson

It is with regret that I have to inform you that I will be withdrawing Will from the school after his GCSEs are completed.

This is not a situation I am happy about, and I am sure nor will Will be when I eventually tell him. Unfortunately, the bullying he has suffered has reached extreme proportions. The timing of this, almost exactly coinciding with my husband running off with a woman he claims was his P.A. (which I can only assume stands for Prostitute / Assistant), thus reducing my allowance dramatically, makes it doubly unfortunate.

I know that you have always said that you wanted parents to alert you immediately at the first sign of bullying, but this came on very quickly and, as said, coinciding but not related to the divorce coming through. Although if the children were making comments to Will about his Dad's new girlfriend looking like an over made-up, cheap-skank whore version of Sharon Stone, I would sympathise.

Will is very much a person to try and work through his problems, and attack them head-on, but on this occasion I have taken the decision out of his hands – I don't want to see him suffer anymore and that's why when we move to our new (smaller) house he'll be going to a comprehensive. In some ways this will be the making of him. I can only imagine the gratitude and respect the comprehensive school children will feel when they meet someone as go-getting, outspoken and forthright as Will. I expect if he ever does return to Longford he'll be carried aloft on shell-suited shoulders.

This is, of course, unless we can come to some arrangement over the fees. The bullying is severe, but I'm sure he could take it if our annual contribution was lower. Getting what it's worth, if you will. I think he'd put up with the bullying; in fact, I'd make sure he did.

I'm sorry for rambling on, but as you know my husband used to deal with all issues of money. Now he's gone, it's left to me. I know we've only met twice, but both times you were very attentive and I'm hoping we can find some way round this terrible mess.

Best wishes,

Polly McKenzie ☺

Polly McKenzie

Personal statement worksheet

| Student Name | William McKenzie |

This section if for your personal statement. Give evidence of the skills you have that are required to study your chosen subject or attain your elected occupation and how you intend to use the knowledge and experience you will gain. Take care to include details of hobbies, interests and any positions of responsibility held and make specific reference to any relevant jobs, placements or work experience undertaken. 4,000 characters max.

Your course

Why are you applying for your chosen course(s)?

Dear Sir or Madam,

Firstly, may I thank you for taking the time to read my personal statement from the no doubt thousands of applications your fine institution must receive at this time of year. May I also add that I consider yours to be one of the finest universities in the country admitting only the best and brightest students. As such, I think you and I are a perfect match.

I should imagine you have probably spent the last few weeks trawling through thousands of UCAS applications desperately looking for something unique: a student whose experience, enthusiasm and drive sets him (or her!) apart.

Well, look no more because I am that student! As you'll see below, I have all the academic and extra curricular prerequisites to instantly place me somewhere near the top of your applicant shortlist. But I also have a unique third quality which I know is desired by universities like yours: I can help with your quotas. Because I go to a state school.

A quick glance over my achievements and predicted grades might lead you to believe you're looking at a public school applicant – and in fact that is partly true. I was educated at Longford School for boys until the age of sixteen, at which point some circumstances outside of my control (and ironically resulting from my father's own LACK of control) meant I had to move to the less financially-draining Rudge Park Comprehensive. And that's my secret weapon! Look, what I'm trying to say is this: if you let me in, I'll get what I want (a return to top-tier education), you'll get what you want (a keen and dedicated thinker) AND you'll also get a tick in the box for state-school applicants, which will look great come league-table time.

continued overleaf.

Every text or MMS I have ever sent has had correct grammar and punctuation and I have never shortened a word, such as "thnx" (that's the first time. Makes me shudder just typing it). I have never and will never, ever use a smiley or winky face. Sadly, it seems these days this alone should mark me out from your other applicants.

While your decision will now hopefully be straightforward, I've still listed my ambitions and achievements below for completeness.

Yours faithfully,

William McKenzie

Your course

Why are you applying for your chosen course(s)?

ELECTED SUBJECT

The subject I wish to study is Philosophy, Politics and Economics. This is because I would like to follow in the footsteps of such influential luminaries as President Obama, the Rt. Hon. Michael Foot and Evan Davis (in his capacity as economist, not presenter of *Dragons' Den*. Although I would maybe consider the latter.).

Why do you think you're suitable for the course(s)?

HOBBIES AND INTERESTS

My interests are legion, but include: literature, the arts, music (both classical and contemporary, especially Crowded House), and roller coasters; I am a "thrill seeker" by nature and, as such, a fully paid-up member of the Roller Coaster Enthusiasts of Great Britain Society. I also like to socialise and have fun (in a responsible and controlled manner, obviously).

POSITIONS OF RESPONSIBILITY

At my previous school, Longford's, I was chairman of the debating society for a short while and a keen amateur dramatist – appearing in no fewer than three productions (of *The Wind In The Willows* and all on successive nights. I played a guard.). No sooner had I moved to Rudge Park than I was elected chairman of the school Christmas Prom committee. I also temporarily and single-handedly managed a care home for the elderly as part of my Duke of Edinburgh Award. Please note: don't contact the home for a reference, they are very busy.

I am also a leader of men. I give you my word on that.

Skills and achievements

Universities like to know the skills you have that will help you on the course, or generally with life at university, like any accredited or non-accredited achievements.

WORK PLACEMENT

I endured a fortnight's work placement as trainee mechanic at Jim's Motors. But rather than view this as "work experience" per se, I prefer to think of it the same way people do about gap years. After all, I experienced what life is like for the underprivileged whilst selflessly helping those less fortunate than me, all the while tolerating inhumane working conditions. It was a character building exercise, of that you can be sure. And I can jump start a battery.

Rudge Park Comprehensive School
Work Experience Feedback Form

Student name: William McKenzie

Company: Jim's Motors

What were the student's strengths?

"strength" isn't a word I'd associate with Will. He's pretty weedy. Could barely lift a hub cap. Wolfie hammered him every single lunch time in the arm-wrestling competition. And they're both the same age, so it's a fair comparison.

What were the student's weaknesses?

As already mentioned, one weakness was that the he was physically weak. Also, he didn't have any relevant qualifications (not even a BTEC in Car maintenance, like Steve). Plus his banter was poor. Honesty was a problem too — seems he's a bit of a fantasist when it comes to his personal life. But worst of the lot, his tea was shit. Way too milky.

What are the student's areas for improvement?

In future, Will to learn how to put less milk in people's tea. And he should stop being such a a specky virgin.

Name and position for the organisation:

Jim, head mechanic.

What did you enjoy about your placement?

Not applicable.

What didn't you enjoy about your placement?

Unfortunately, there appears to be insufficient space in this allotted area to write down all the things I didn't enjoy, but I'll give it a go anyway. I didn't enjoy: the childish initiation ceremony which resulted in me being stripped, institutionally bullied and very nearly drowned; the unsanitary, and quite possibly illegal, condition of the staff toilet; the intrusion into my social life outside of work hours; the pathetic nicknames which my temporary colleagues bestowed upon me; being forced to work shoulder-to-shoulder

with, well, basically, savages. Essentially, the answer to the question "What didn't you enjoy about your placement?" is "everything".

What did you learn from your work experience?

I learnt two things. Firstly, I learnt about the inherent flaws in the school's work experience scheme which can all too easily result in students being placed in utterly inappropriate work arenas. Secondly, I learnt that when it comes to the female chest, working-class men prefer big round bouncy ones over petite pert little ones. Revelatory, I think you'll agree.

Has your work experience aided your career choices?

My work experience has aided my career choices by strengthening my already pretty strong resolution to never, ever gain employment as a manual labourer. To put it bluntly, I am much cleverer than you need to be to work in such places and, when you think about it, if clever people took all the manual jobs what would stupid people do to earn money? That would be irresponsible and so, in a way, I'm helping those less fortunate than I.

Signature of student:

William McKenzie

Form: WEL6001 back

Rudge Park Comprehensive School

Student end of year report: Deputy Head's assessment

Student name: WILLIAM McKENZIE   Year: 6th Form

Ah yes, young William. William McKenzie. The boy has a unique outlook on life and certain behavioural quirks that I'm sure any one of these so-called 'educational psychologists' would be only too happy to label a syndrome, albeit very slowly and over several sessions whilst charging an extortionate hourly rate. But don't worry, it's not a syndrome, he's just very overly keen — and that can easily be interpreted as a mental disorder.

Over the last two years I've spent several long, long minutes in McKenzie's company. Not out of choice, but because he is hellbent on being "involved" with the goings on at the school. I have taught literally hundreds of pupils in my time, yet none have been as obsessively ambitious as McKenzie. While most of his contemporaries exhibit normal, non-strange behaviours, Will seems to misunderstand that extra-curricular activities are optional, and signs up for them like they are going out of fashion.

He went to great lengths to ensure that he was elected Chairman of Rudge Park's first (and last) ever Christmas disco. The following term, Will gleefully accepted the role of year representative for Rudge Park's first (and last) foray into the increasingly irrelevant

Signature:

Continuation:

world of the Duke of Edinburgh Awards Scheme, a role so manifestly meaningless I'm staggered even he accepted. Yet I can't think of anyone more deserving of such a vacuous position than serial teacher-botherer McKenzie.

Being totally honest, it does slightly irk me that academically, Will has done pretty well. Despite receiving shocking AS level results (due to an unfortunate medical incident in the exam hall) his A-Level predictions are boringly good. But ultimately, if it helps the league table stats, then tolerating a couple of years of his kind of relentless, unhealthy enthusiasm and interference is an almost fair price to pay.

But let's look to the future. While I can't honestly say the school community has benefited from McKenzie's presence, it will most certainly not suffer from him leaving. It will mostly be indifferent, I'd imagine.

However, I hate to say it, but I actually think I'm going to miss him. In the way that a boxer prefers to lay into a punch bag rather than merely shadow box, I'm going to miss "talking" to him and "discussing" ideas with him. I'm going to miss his bespectacled know-it-all face interrupting me with inconsequential mutterings when I'm trying to work. They really don't make them like McKenzie anymore, but there are probably very good reasons for this, such as social evolution.

Signature:

P. Gilbert.

REVISION SCHEDULE - JUNE

MONDAY 1	TUESDAY 2	WEDNESDAY 3	THUR
Revise "Culture & Identity"	Re-revise "Culture & Identity"	Re-re-revise "Culture & Identity"	RELAXATION DAY
Revise "Modern Britain"	Re-revise "Modern Britain"	Re-re-revise "Modern Britain"	Allow brain cells to recharge by focusing on non-exam based thoughts: Read "An Inspector Calls" for fun.
Drink two cans of energy drink.	Drink two cans of energy drink	Drink two cans of energy drink	
Read "Tess of the D'Urbervilles	Re-read "Tess of the D'Urbervilles"	Re-re-read "Tess of the D'Urbervilles"	Drink two cans of energy drink to stimulate relaxation

Revise tomorrow due to lie-in

Revise tomorrow due to lie-in

START WEEK 1 REVISION

Room needed tidying

TESS

FRIDAY 5	SATURDAY 6	SUNDAY 7	
Energy drink breakfast	Search for previous exam papers online	Write sample answers to last year's exam papers for all subjects, and mark these sample answers myself	SOCIOLOGY
			POLITICS
Test myself on "Culture & Identity"			ENGLISH LITERATURE
Revise "PM Powers and Limitations"			
			ALL SUBJECTS
1x Pro Plus for evening revision.			
			PHYSICAL SUSTENANCE
Read "An Inspector Calls" for revision.			
			MENTAL SUSTENANCE

Revise Culture and Identity

REVISE:
C + ID
MOD. BRIT
TESS !!

Buy Pro Plus?

...distracted will be imposing an internet ban on myself from tomorrow onwards

NOTE TO SELF: STOP PANICKING

No Rest
Read the rest OF TESS OF THE D'URBEVILLES

WEEK 2
Revise every-thing from LAST WEEK ± ALL NEW = STUFF!

(Read rest of Jane Eyre)

MONDAY 8	TUESDAY 9	WEDNESDAY 10	THURSDAY 11
Drink two cans of energy drink	Drink two cans of energy drink	Drink two cans of energy drink	**RELAXATION DAY**
Record audio notes on "Welfare"	Listen subliminally to audio notes on "Welfare" while sleeping	Test self on subliminal learnings from audio notes on "Welfare"	Watch Paul McKenna's "Mind Workout for A-Level Revision" DVD
Drink two cans of energy drink	Drink two cans of energy drink	Drink two cans of energy drink	Drink only one can of energy drink
Write post it notes on "US Foreign Policy"	Stick "US Foreign Policy" notes on bathroom walls to read whilst on toilet.	Spend three hours on toilet to absorb "US Foreign Policy" notes	Gaming treat: Play Dr Kowashima's Brain Training on DS
1x Pro Plus	1x Pro Plus	1x Pro Plus	
Read "Jane Eyre"	Cut out each individual page in "Jane Eyre"	x pages to my room walls, floor and ceiling to form a learning collage of "Jane Eyre"	

Computer kept crashing so took all day to record notes

READ FUCKING TESS!!!

Read Jane Eyre

CULTURE + ID
MOD. BRIT.
·TESS·!!
INSR CALLS
PM. POWERS
Pro Plus!!!

FRIDAY 12	SATURDAY 13	SUNDAY 14	
Search for leaked upcoming exam papers online	Investigate consequences of illegally obtaining upcoming exam papers	**REVISION SCHEDULE REVIEW**	SO...
Drink two cups of chamomile tea to sooth anxiety;		Spend eight hours reviewing this revision schedule; evaluate success up until this point and apply findings to subsequent days in this revision schedule	PO...
drink two cans of energy drink to balance out the tea			ENG. LITERATURE
Redraw, from memory, the "Jane Eyre" wall collage			ALL SUBJECTS
			PHYSICAL SUSTENANCE
			MENT... SUSTE...

Distracted again. Internet ban reinstated

Internet ban will definitely Start tomorrow

→ See Doctor about stomach tomorrow
→ Look up symptoms on the internet (LIFT BAN)
→ US Foreign Policy.

...evise U.S. ...reign Policy ...nd skip Lunch.

U.S. FOREIGN → POLICY

TESS, TESS, TESS

START REVISING CULTURE AND IDENTITY

Note: only three hours sleep tonight. To catch up on last two weeks revision

RIGHT - REVISION BEGINS IN EARNEST:
MODERN BRITAIN/
TESS / PM POWERS/
CULTURE + IDENTITY/
FAMILY + COMMUNITY/
IS THERE ANYTHING ELSE?

	TUESDAY 16	WEDNESDAY 17	THURSDAY 18
Write index card notes on "Family and Community"

Drink four cans of energy drink

Highlight all important elements on "The United Nations" in politics textbook- in yellow

2x Pro Plus

Read "Arcadia"

Tried reading in the shower. Books got wet | Get Mum to do a fun quiz with me on "Family and Community" using index cards

Drink five cans of energy drink

Highlight all unimportant elements on "The United Nations" in politics textbook - in pink

2x Pro Plus

Act out "Arcadia", playing all the parts myself, video performance

Replace showering time with revision time | Summerise index cards on "Family and Community" and write questions about those summaries

Drink seven cans of energy drink

Notate "The United Nations" in politics textbook in red pen

2.5x Pro Plus

Watch back video of "Arcadia" performance | Get Mum to invigilate a mock exam based on my "Family and Community" questions - living room?

No Energy drink for health reasons

Drink seven espressos

Highlight key notations in "The United Nations" in politics textbook - green

5x Pro Plus (to compensate for lack of energy drink)

Record audio from "Arcadia" video to iPod for further subliminal learning

OVERSLEPT. |

TESS / CULTURE T.V / INSPECTOR CALLS / PM POWERS / ARCADIA/ UN / CHECK OUT YOUTUBE??? / US. F. POLICY

FRIDAY 19	SATURDAY 20	SUNDAY 21	
Search for leaked upcoming exam answers online

As per 18th | Search for the names of Exam Board members online, Google their names to see where they live - if local, consider ways to surreptitiously fraternise with them and get onto subject of ideal exam answers

As per 19th | Scan job websites for careers available to those candidates who only have GCSEs

RELAXATION AFTERNOON:

Make YouTube playlist of lectures on Arcadia / Jane Eyre / An Inspector Calls / Tess D'Urbervilles

Watch YouTube playlist. | |

MOD. BRIT Will I remember ANY OF this ??

NOTHING'S GOING FUCKING. IN

REVISION SCHEDULE - JUNE

of PRO-PLUS

Distracted by Sivan and Neil coming over. Also had to buy a crate of energy drinks and 12 packs

MONDAY 22	TUESDAY 23	WEDNESDAY 24	THUR...
Two espressos	Create a "Micro Revision" schedule to focus on knowledge gaps	Two espressos	VISUALISATION DAY
Prepare list of gaps in Sociology knowledge		"Micro revise" Sociology knowledge gaps	Spend several hours contemplating what success will look like. Imagine what three A's will taste like; savour the taste
Drink six cans of energy drink.	CATCH UP IN ALL SUBJECTS	Drink six cans of energy drink	
Prepare list of gaps in Politics knowledge		"Micro Revise" gaps in Politics knowledge	
3x Pro Plus	POLITICS*	3x Pro Plus	
Prepare list of gaps in English Literature knowledge		"Micro Revise" gaps in English Literature knowledge	*Overslept. And internet ban properly reinstated as of today!*

Skip meals, washing and sleep to catch up.

READ **TESS** LAST CHANCE

WIKIPEDIA?

FRIDAY 26	SATURDAY 27	SUNDAY 28	SO...
Revise everything in all subjects	Re-revise everything in all subjects	FINAL 24 HOUR REVISION PUSH	POLITICS
EVERY-THING	If pressure is getting too much and becoming mentally crippling, consider "alternatives" to completing exams. There is ALWAYS a way out; write the "note" and organise affairs, just in case	Drink eight cans of energy drink to push on through the pain barrier	ENGLISH LITERATURE
		Listen exclusively to my "Calming Debussy" playlist.	ALL SUBJECTS
		Revisit the "note" from yesterday and make final decision. If it still makes sense, do what needs to be done.	PHYSICAL SUSTENA...
			MENTAL SUSTENA...

POLITICS
ENG. LIT

SOCIOLOGY Help.

ALTERNATIVES ??→

PRO PLUS

FINAL PUSH →

REVISIO DULE - JUNE

MONDAY 29	~~SDAY 30~~ TUESDAY 30
SOCIOLOGY EXAM 10am-12:30pm	Breakfast: seed based granola, two cans of energy drink
If exam went really badly, have one more look at the "note"	ENGLISH LITERATURE EXAM, 11am- 1:45pm
Look up the answers to the difficult questions from the previous exam. Castigate self	Power lunch: seeds, bottle of Pomegreat and three cans of energy drink
Revise English Literature and Politics throughout the night - no sleep permitted	Three minutes' silent reflection
Drink eight cans of energy drink with eight Pro Plus to ensure maximum revision time.	POLITICS EXAM, 2pm- 5pm
	Celebrate with half a dozen vodka and energy drinks

Didn't get to sleep till 5am.

SOCIOLOGY

POLITICS

ENGLISH LITERATURE

ALL SUBJECTS

PHYSICAL SUSTENANCE

MENTAL SUSTENANCE

REVISION BALANCE STRATEGY

I'm really worried about my stomach

CONFIDENCE

HUMILITY

PHYSICAL CONDITION

FEAR OF FAILURE (39%)

ACADEMIC KNOWLEDGE (38%)

FOCUS DURING EXAM (23%)

Debut Novel Outline
by Will McKenzie

Lead Character Name Ideas
Billy McKenzie? Wilma Kenzie? Bill McKinsey? Will McDonald?

The Synopsis
An epic tale which offers a contemporary take on timeless, human themes: adventure, jealousy, love, revenge and pride.

The hero, Bill McKinsey, is a cultured 19-year-old who is thrust from his aristocratic upbringing into abject poverty. While living amongst the underclasses, he shuns the ways of his sheep-like, trend-following peers and lives by his own, more considered and sensible rules. So by not mindlessly adopting the behaviours of the masses, he is actually more of a rebel than those who would normally be considered rebels. He has a sidekick who is dumb but loyal, a romantic fool but who will fight for Will to the death. Our hero, Will, teaches this loyal fellow of the underclass (Lieman? Dimon?) the ways of being a gentleman, the ways of the world, and ultimately how to be cool and brilliant.

Font
Preferred typeface would be Baskerville, the font which I believe was used in the early editions of James Joyce's *Ulysses*. If it was good enough for him, it's good enough for me.

Page Count
My copy of *Ulysses* comes in at 672 pages. *The Da Vinci Code* comes in at 605. So to ensure my novel receives both critical acclaim (like *Ulysses*) and becomes a bestseller (like *The Da Vinci Code*) I shall aim for the average of these two, which equates to 638.5 pages.

Should The Book Be Published In Hardback?
Yes.

What Will The Book Dedication Be?
"For my Mother, and for C.H."

A subtle but clear snub to my father and a coded declaration of love to Charlotte Hinchcliffe with the underlying subtext, "Look at what you could have had! I've written a bestseller and I've dedicated it to you, but you now can't have me because I'm rich and famous. And now fit, clever journalists with pictures by their names in the paper are throwing themselves at me and I'm having sex with them right back. And I now know what just moving my hips means. And they love the sex. And they also commission me to write book reviews."

(I will anonymously send her a first edition copy to ensure she gets the point.)

ABOUT THE AUTHOR SLEEVE NOTES

"Despite his parents separating during his most crucial and formative years of schooling, William turned adversity into literary success by channelling his fear and sadness into this, his stunning debut novel. With 12 GSCEs (8 A*s, 4 As) already behind him, we are surely witnessing the birth of a truly prodigious talent. William's other interests include roller coasters."

COMPETITIONS TO ENTER THE NOVEL INTO

Booker Prize, Costa Prize, Guardian First Book Award. Not that the latter two count for anything, but might as well go for all three.

OTHER MARKETING IDEAS

- Get the book stocked in both big retailers and upmarket retailers - i.e. Tesco and Waterstones.
- Do book signings – focus on London's Oxford Street bookshops for maximum footfall.
- Investigate whether the Richard and Judy Book Club is still running.
- Get Stephen Fry to tweet that he likes it and include a link to Amazon.

IF YOU HAVE READ THIS FAR THEN I URGE YOU TO TURN YOURSELF INTO A POLICE STATION SO THAT YOU CAN PAY THE PENALTY FOR YOUR INTELLECTUAL PROPERTY THEFT.

EVERYTHING © WILLIAM McKENZIE

Dear Kerry,

Firstly, as we haven't spoken since last week's dramatic events at
Neil's birthday, I would like to start by hoping that you are well and
that you haven't had any other misfortunes to add to the tragic recent
loss of your father.

With the benefit of hindsight, I now see that certain elements of
my behaviour and language that fateful evening may have been
inappropriate and therefore I would like to apologise for some of the
things I said. Not all, but some. Other things just need clarifying in a
rational manner.

For example, I would like to clarify that when I projected across the
room that I had turned down sexual favours from the Empire State
building, I was merely satirising the completely unfair reputation that
some of your peers have bestowed on you with regards to your height
and the likelihood that you will perform certain "acts". So rather than
perpetuating this cruel and unfounded stereotype, I was actually very
cleverly aping their disgusting mentality although, on reflection, I can
see that my outburst may not have been immediately recognisable as
such. For that, I apologise.

I also regret the really very poor timing of my break up announcement.
Actually, I'm not entirely comfortable with using the words "break
up" there as they do imply that we were in a genuine relationship
whereas, technically, we just visited a few places simultaneously and
shared a solitary kiss. Semantics aside, for me to announce this news
at a time when you were still smarting from your Dad's passing was
deeply regrettable. Though not my fault. Because, as we all know,
I was utterly unaware of your recent bereavement because Simon

neglected to pass on this critical piece of trivia to me. Had I known, of course I would never have done something so seemingly callous. In fact, I probably would have had the common decency to just steer clear of you in the first place, to avoid the inevitable complications and drama that result from your "issues".

With the apologies put to bed, I would now like to focus on a couple of points regarding the unfair treatment of me by you and others at Neil's party. Firstly, while your emotions are no doubt all over the place at the moment – which is bound to make you more irrational – I do hope that in the cold light of day you have realised that your father's death and my "breaking up" with you are completely unrelated events. They're different things. It's like comparing apples with bananas (not that your dead Dad is in anyway like a banana). But by unjustly and illogically combining the two events, you publicly implied that I was some kind of insensitive barbarian. And I resent that because I'm not. Just look at this letter, not many people would send such a sensitive clarification.

Which brings me to my second point. If I were an insensitive barbarian, then I can promise you I would have waited until after you'd performed a certain "act" on me before "breaking up" with you. I did not do that. No. Instead, I behaved in a gentlemanly fashion and sacrificed my own carnal pleasure in the name of your honour. And the reward for my selfless act? My reputation mauled in public and me getting barred from Neil's house.

Now that I have provided you with a much more balanced perspective on things and you are no doubt starting to feel embarrassed about the way you behaved, I would just like to say that I forgive you. But please, please, please do not feel obliged to write a letter of apology in return, or to communicate to your peers / social group that you unfairly slandered me and that your actions were a kind of temporary insanity brought on by grief.

Honestly, please. You have so much going on in your life at the
moment that I don't want to add to your burden even if, in normal
circumstances, those would probably be the appropriate things to
do. That said, if you do decide to go with an apology letter / wider
communication concerning misinformation, it might be better to
wait a few months till you're off those heavy anti-depressants so that
people don't think it's just the drugs talking.

I hold no grudge against you Kerry and wish you all the best in
your future relationships. Not that what we had was a relationship,
obviously.

Yours sincerely,

Will McKenzie

William McKenzie

PS. I return a picture you gave me – not that I didn't want it, it's just
that it's yours.

COLLECTED WORKS

By JOHN WEBSTER

Art Editor

Firstly, thank you to yearbook editor Will McKenzie for allowing me to exhibit some of my works of art on these pages. I have always felt a special kinship with Will, as we not only started on the same day but he also gave me the greatest honour of my school career by appointing me head of prom catering. He's made my life worthwhile. Thank you Will.

As you will all have already seen my A-Level artwork in the corridor next to the dining room, I have decided to showcase some of my personal art here – all pieces I have done in my spare time at home.

I hope you enjoy them and if you are interested in purchasing any of the originals, they are available for sale with prices starting at £4.50.

John

Comfort

My counsellor said I should draw something that comforted me. And that's why I drew this picture and called it "Comfort". When I look at this picture, I feel reassured. Here are the other things I think of when I see this picture: Hunger. Sadness. Cheestrings.

You Cannot Control Me

We are all kings and queens of our own domains and we must recognise who holds the power within our kingdoms and queendoms. This advice was given to me by my counsellor and it made me think a lot – so I turned it into this picture. I hope you like it.

Friends In Another Multiverse

This is a very personal picture. It is a portrait of someone who is very similar to me. He doesn't really talk to me, but I often imagine that in another parallel multiverse he does talk to me. And I imagine that in that multiverse we are able to discuss our mutual pain with each other. Who knows, maybe he'll see this picture and he'll become my friend in this multiverse.

Look At Me!

We are all striving to be important to someone, according to my counsellor. Some people play sport to get attention. Some shout insulting names at you about your size, mental health or haircut to get attention. Others just sit quietly, hoping that one day someone will notice them and that, just for that one moment, they won't feel invisible anymore.

Frustration – A Self-Portrait

Most people's frustration is born out of not feeling they are special. No one likes to be put in the corner and ignored. But if we really want to be noticed, not just within our schools but internationally, there is always something we can do. It just depends on how hard the popular people push you.

THOUGHTS FROM THE EDITOR

What Can Rudge Park Learn?

At first this sounds like an odd question doesn't it? Surely we come to a school to be taught, so how can a school itself actually learn? Well, I believe that my generation owes it to future Rudge Park pupils to build a better school for them. And this yearbook seems like an appropriate place to reflect and feed back on the elements of the school which could be improved.

Us pupils have lived and breathed this school for some time now, so we know its strengths and weaknesses better than anyone. I'm sure that every single one of us has ideas on how the school could improve and with this spirit of collaboration in mind, I put a notice on the sixth form pin-board inviting suggestions. Sadly, after two weeks, it remained untouched save for the statutory ejaculating penis, so I have decided to handle the issue by myself.

As a relative newcomer to the school, I do have significant experience of high-level education outside of Rudge Park and as such am uniquely positioned to not only identify problem areas, but also offer constructive solutions.

So, this generation of Rudge Parkians (mainly me) will now lay down the gauntlet to the teachers and administrative staff; if you care about our legacy, then please take these suggestions seriously.

WILLIAM McKENZIE

Rudge Park Yearbook Chairman and Editor and former private school pupil

Societies and Clubs

In this era of measurability, school league tables are clearly important, but exam grades are only one part of producing exceptional, well-rounded pupils. At my old school, Longford School for Boys, there was a lot of focus on what they referred to as "other half" activities; things other than classroom lessons. Here at Rudge Park we currently have five clubs and societies (Football, Orchestra, Art Club [incorporating Art Club Overflow], Chess Club, Greco-Roman Wrestling). Compare this to the number of clubs and societies laid on by Longford School For Boys in this extract from their prospectus:

The clubs and societies available over the autumn term at Longford School For Boys include:

SPORTS

Rugby, Cross Country, Fives, Chess, Croquet, Eton Fives, Table Tennis, Athletics, Bridge, Multigym, Korfball, Real Tennis, Rugby Fives, Badminton, Sailing, Ultimate Frisbee, Rowing, Basketball, Windsurfing, Squash, Netball For Boys, Football, Skiing, Swimming, Fencing, Volley Ball, Rock Climbing, Lacrosse, Rackets, Golf.

CLUBS

First Orchestra, Second Orchestra, Third Orchestra, First Wind Band, Second Wind Band, Brass Band, Chamber Choir, Clarinet Ensemble, Debating Society, Model Railway Society, Film Society, Cookery, Jazz Improvisation Group, Classics Society, Bridge Club, Wargaming Society, Etiquette Club, Dance Club, Theatre Design and Tech Crew, Dickens Society, Ceramics Club, Economics Society, Young Enterprise, Sixth form Historical Film Club, Cadets, Poetry Club, Historical Re-enactment Society, Lower School Website Design Club, Physics Club, Voluntary Club, Art Club.

That's 62 in total – and that's just autumn term! I'm not saying that Rudge Park needs that many, but an extra half dozen clubs (say Debating, Sailing, Real Tennis, Bridge, Fencing and Historical Re-enactment) would be a start. Finding the time for these additional activities in the timetable may be tough, but if there's no give in the current schedule perhaps Saturday morning school could be considered? A sacrifice, yes, but surely one worth taking if it results in a better all-round education?

Field Trips

While a lot was learned on this year's Geography and Sociology field trip to Swanage, I do feel that Rudge Park could look further afield. As we now live in a global village, it would be valuable for students here to have a bit more of a global perspective rather than only ever travelling within a 100 mile radius of Rudge Park, and even then, only in one direction.

Compare Swanage to this list of excursions:

FIELD TRIP ITINERARY FOR THE UPCOMING YEAR

OCTOBER: Classics Trip (*Rome, Pompeii, Athens*)

NOVEMBER: Business Studies & Economics Trip (*Singapore*)

DECEMBER: Voluntary Society Trip to Botswana

JANUARY: Rugby Tour of South Africa

FEBRUARY: Ski Tour (*Whistler, Canada*)

MARCH: Sailing Society Excursion (*South Africa*)

APRIL: Geography Field Trip (*Reykjavik*)

MAY: Sixth Form Inca Trail Trek

JUNE: Lower School Geography Field Trip (*Swanage*)

That itinerary is from the prospectus of my former school, Longford School for Boys. Fair enough, they did go to Swanage as well, something I only noticed after I glued in the extract. But the point remains the same; for Rudge Park pupils to become worldlier, they must be shown more of the world. Budgetary constraints are obviously an issue, but I would imagine that lottery funding is available for this kind of venture – or if not, some kind of private investment must surely be possible?

Summary

So, I return to the initial funny-sounding question that I posed in the title of this article: "What Can Rudge Park Learn?" Well, based on learnings from other institutions, I would propose that Rudge Park:

- Considers the addition of Saturday morning school

and

- Investigates methods of private funding

Don't thank me; thank the system that made me.

SETHI

Timeless!

Timeless styling with Jasdeep's own modern twist.

Extra Jazzy!

For that extra-special occasion!

After all, true style never goes out of fashion.

Contemporary!

"I think it's kind of hideous. Is it velvet?" another satisfied customer "Will that be okay to print in your advert?" Mr A. Cooper

So for the jazziest suits in all of Great Britain, visit Jasdeep Sethi today!

Shuttlecock Whackers

Fellow whackers,

Like this gorgeous weather we're having, Wednesday night club nights are really hotting up with some serious action both on and off court. The first team men are pushing their way ever deeper into the Surrey League despite strong resistance from a strongly-tipped Woking side and there's been some eye-watering four-way action with the mixed doubles.

The seconds got a vigorous seeing-to at the hands of some rugged-looking lads from Chertsey which, alas, I was unable to observe, and I'm pleased to report the third team men are making a good fist of things. However, my eye's firmly on the under 17 boys who are looking remarkably fresh going into the playoffs, though I've heard that despite a last-minute comeback from the Ringwood Racketeers which put the willies up our lads, they then came from behind to finish things off in a truly thrilling climax. I wasn't around to see that either, which is a shame.

Off the courts, I'm pleased to report that my Tom Cruise movie season was brought to a rousing finish with last Monday's showing of *Cocktail* in the club bar. My own drinks creations were unfortunately less well received, although after everyone had left, I did manage to convince the chairman to take one from me.

One further thing worth mentioning is that the club is actively looking for new joiners. Whether you're a total beginner, occasional tickler or an experienced shuttlecock basher it's always a pleasure to swell the members. Application forms available at the bar. I would love you to fill one in for me.

Until my next little update, play well and maybe I'll see you for a whack on court, if not in the clubhouse afterwards. Mine's a Drambuie!

Yours,

Kevin Sutherland
Club Secretary

Tit Mountain

WILL

SIMON

ME

JAY

WELL
THAT'S
a bit
gay NIEL

SHUT JAY
UP

COULDN'T
SAID IT
GO DOWN
SINCE HE
TESTED
COCK ENLARGERS
FOR NASA

I feel
really
bad about
that fish ☺

HELP!

ANGRY
STAIN

RAHHH! Boobs